THE

WILL THORNE
GENERAL SECRETARY NATIONAL UNION
OF GASWORKERS. &. GENERAL LABOURERS
1889

The Air of Freedom:

The Birth of The New Unionism

Yvonne Kapp

LAWRENCE & WISHART
LONDON

Lawrence & Wishart Limited
144a Old South Lambeth Road
London SW8 1XX

First published 1989

Photoset in North Wales by
Derek Doyle & Associates, Mold, Clwyd
Printed and bound in Great Britain at
The Camelot Press plc, Southampton

Contents

Illustrations

Illustrations

Sources

Illustrations, 2, 6, 7, 10, 20, 29, 30, 31, 32, 33, 34, 38, 39, 40
by courtesy of London Gas Museum
Illustrations 8, 28, 36 by courtesy of East Midland Gas
Museum
Illustrations 12, 18, 19, 21 by courtesy of Communist Party
Library
Illustrations 4, 15 by courtesy of Science Museum, London

Acknowledgments

My thanks to John Edmonds, General Secretary of the GMB, for inviting me to undertake the congenial task of writing these centenary notes; to Peter Carter, Director of Studies at the GMB College, for his unstinting help in providing me with material; and to Betty Lewis for additional archives and research assistance.

I owe an immense debt of gratitude to Derek Matthews – not personally known to me – for his excellent unpublished Ph.D. thesis, *The London Gasworks: A Technical, Commercial and Labour History until 1914*, which has been an invaluable source of information.

Yvonne Kapp
London 1988

Foreword

On 31 March 1889 modern trade unionism was born in Britain.

Until Will Thorne and Ben Tillett made their challenging call to gasworkers in the East End of London, only skilled workers were organised in trade unions. That historic meeting in Canning Town founded a new union and generated an energy that surged through the working people of Britain. Within a year Will Thorne had helped the dockers to win a memorable victory, and branches of unskilled and low paid union members were formed throughout the country. Trade unionism broke free from the conservatism of the old crafts and aspired to be a mass movement.

Will Thorne symbolised the new spirit. He grew up in poverty, had no schooling and was put to work as soon as he could earn a penny. Yet he dragged himself out of the oppressive heat of the retort house and led his members to achieve the first success of the new unionism – the eight-hour day for gasworkers at Beckton.

The story of the foundation of our union should inspire every GMB member. We complain of government hostility and legal attack, but our predecessors overcame many greater obstacles. Without education or welfare support or political influence, and in the face of brutal opposition from almost every employer, they won the right to organise and began the long struggle to achieve justice and dignity for working people.

This book records the pioneering triumph of the founders of the GMB. It is a well told tale of ordinary men and women which with its many pictures of working people should make this a lasting monument to them. We can best honour their memory by continuing their work.

John Edmonds
November 1988

Preface

Many more people than are mentioned in this brief sketch were involved in the founding of the Gasworkers' Union. It goes without saying that so vigorous a movement could never have come into being – let alone thrive and prosper for a hundred years – without the active participation of countless staunch men and women, some of whom became prominent as national or regional officials, many thousands upon thousands of others remaining forever anonymous.

Similarly, this account is strongly centred upon London, which is where it all began. Nevertheless it is clear that the organisation would not have flourished unless it had rapidly taken root throughout Britain and Ireland, where its members made their own history over the years.

To all these people the GMB today owes a tremendous debt, which it daily repays by increasing the union's strength and influence and, above all, by playing a leading part, as did its founders, in responding to the needs of its time.

It is not surprising that the revolution created by the establishing of the first general workers' union should have been overshadowed for many contemporary chroniclers by the Dock Strike which, nearly six months after the success of the gasworkers, brought the commerce of London to a standstill. What seems curious is that social historians ever since – including the most recent who have access to all the evidence – have largely chosen to ignore the gasworkers of 1889 who were the prime cause, the model and the stimulus for other labouring men, to the abiding merit of its founders.

I

The Founders

Sunday morning, March 31st 1889 – a lovely sunny
morning – was the birthday of the National Union of
Gas Workers and General Labourers of Great
Britain and Ireland …

In those words, nearly 25 years later, Will
Thorne recorded the founding of the great trade
union which, renamed the National Union of
General Workers in 1916, grew to become the
National Union of General and Municipal
Workers in 1924, the General, Municipal,
Boilermakers and Allied Trades Union in 1983
and is today known as the GMB: the second
largest union in the land.

Now, on its centenary, we look back to its
remarkable beginnings at the Gas, Light &
Coke company's Beckton works, built – in 1868
and at a cost of £100,000 two miles beyond the
outskirts of London – by the engineer Frederick
John Evans on 150 acres of windswept Essex
marshland near Galleon's Reach. The land had

been bought from the Worshipful Company of Ironmongers – one of the twelve ancient livery companies – for £150,000 and was named after the Governor of what was then familiarly known as the Chartered company, Simon Adams Beck, whose father, James, was the clerk to the Ironmongers and a solicitor who had negotiated the sale.

The gasworks went into production in November 1870. At the time they were the largest in England – indeed, in the world – employing over 3,000 men. Within a year, however, they had to be extended still further, the number of retort houses – built after the fashion of the great vaulted railway stations of the day – being increased from four to eight.

Will Thorne

In one of these Will Thorne had worked as a stoker since 1885. He was then 28 having been born in 1857 – the eldest of four children and the only boy – in Farm Street, Hockley, a suburb of Birmingham: the city where William Murdoch, one of the earliest British gas engineers, first displayed his invention by illuminating the frontage of Boulton & Watt's Soho factory to mark the (very temporary) Peace of Amiens in 1802.

Thanks to Thorne's latest – French –

No.9 Retort House, Beckton, 1881

biographer, it is now known that his father, Thomas, was a widower of 35 when he married Emma Everess, then twenty. Their small back-to-back house stood in a mean street, eventually demolished to make way for a factory upon whose wall a plaque commemorates Will's birthplace.

Both his father and his mother worked in the brickfields, as their parents had done before them and, like many of his kind, Thomas Thorne, a red-clay brickmaker, regularly went south when summer came, returning in the autumn to earn his living as a stoker in the Saltley gasworks, owned by Birmingham Corporation, on the eastern outskirts of the city.

A hard worker and a hard drinker, he died as a result of one of his many fights when Will was seven years old, having been struck on the head by a man later tried and sentenced for manslaughter. Even before that calamity the small boy had started work, turning a wheel for a rope-spinner twelve hours a day on five days of the week and seven hours on the sixth day for 2s 6d (12½p).

Since he was of an age when our children are barely out of their second year at primary school it would be agreeable to suppose that little Will Thorne was at least free to play during the weekend but, on the contrary, he was sent to his uncle's barber shop as lather boy

Plaque on factory wall of Joseph Lucas Ltd, King Street, Birmingham

until eleven o'clock on Saturday nights and again on Sunday mornings until two. For this he was paid 1 shilling (5p).

Eventually the rope-spinner threatened to reduce his pittance of a wage, whereupon the child rebelled and left the job. That 'first strike', he wrote in after years, was never settled, for he simply did not go back. The widowed mother took whatever work she could get but with three small children under six – one not yet a year old – it had to be done in the home. She spent her days and many of her nights, helped by a sister, sewing pearl buttons on to cards: twelve to a card. For a gross of these she earned three ha'pence, out of which she had to buy her needles and thread. In this desperate poverty she applied for relief to the Board of Guardians who granted her the bounty of 4 shillings and four loaves of bread each week. Young Will was sent every Wednesday to collect this bene-faction, walking two miles to and from the Poor Law offices. Tuesdays, he wrote, were days of fasting for the five of them.

The exercise could be regarded as training for his next job which was three miles from his home in a brick and tile works. Here, starting at six in the morning and lasting for twelve hours, he handled several tons of bricks in the course of each day. It was, indeed, such heavy toil that his wage was raised from 7 to 8 shillings, since he was doing 'a man's work'. Later he was put to tending at night the kilns where the bricks were fired, for which he earned an extra shilling; but, after spending two consecutive nights without rest, he fell asleep on the third night at four in the morning and was sacked. This was his first experience of being out of work. He was not yet nine years old.

His next job was again in a brickfield where, as before, he had to fetch and carry heavy loads for his master: in this instance an exceptionally fast worker with a short temper who repeatedly struck the boy whenever he was kept waiting for material. There was an even longer walk to this job at the start and end of the tiring day: he had to rise in the early hours of the morning, as did his mother who insisted upon getting his breakfast before dawn. The strain upon them both proved too great and Mrs Thorne, though she would badly miss her boy's 8 shillings a week, made him give up the work.

After another bout of unemployment he went as a general handyman to a plumber and tinsmith. That lasted the best part of a year, after which he took on various jobs, including the 'rather unpleasant occupation', as he mildly called it, of going round butchers' shops to pick up cows' and pigs' hairs which, after treatment, were sold to plasterers and wig-makers.

He was now pushing fourteen, had taught himself swimming in the local canal and was strong, though not tall, for his age. It was the time of the Franco-Prussian war and he found work in a metal-rolling and ammunition factory: 'this little hell on earth', as he called it.

> The roar and the rattle, the steam and the heat of that inferno remains vivid in my memory, and many times I have dreamt of that place, waking up in a sweat of fear.

He not only remembered it but also bore the physical scars of that experience all the days of his life, for the acids of the pickling tubs which corroded his clothes ate into the flesh of his hands, 'to the very bone', as he put it.

For almost a year he was on the twelve-hour nightshift, never seeing sunlight, and it was then that he swore he would do anything he could

> to help prevent other children going through the same hardships, misery and suffering ... We were poor ignorant victims of a system that made us work long hours of brutalising toil for little pay; a system that had no care for the slums we slept in, the food we ate, or the education we received ...

It was while in this engineering factory that he took part in his second strike. The men in the strip and metal-rolling shops demanded a pay rise and were refused. The strike that followed was dealt with in a manner that was to

become very familiar to Thorne in after years:
scabs were brought in to replace the strikers,
though in this instance they were given short
shrift and most of them decided it was more
prudent to keep away.

As with other forms of unemployment, being
on strike presented the problem of too much
leisure and no money. Young Thorne and his
workmates pawned their boots and other
clothing to buy drinks and they kicked their
heels in pubs and hung about the streets. They
were glad enough to go back to work when the
strike was settled in the workers' favour.
Thorne recorded that this was his 'earliest
lesson in the law of supply and demand': to
fulfil the profitable orders enabling Frenchmen
and Germans to kill each other had outweighed
the firm's urge to keep down wages.

That was not the only lesson he learnt here,
for he had his first taste of blatant injustice. He
was taken off a job for which he earned 18
shillings a week in order that it might be done
by the foreman's brother who, however, was
paid 22 shillings. The brothers then fell out,
and Thorne was put back on the job, but at 18
shillings. His protests were of no avail: on the
contrary, they earned him the sack.

Now, at sixteen, he took on a variety of more
or less unskilled work – on railway wagons, in
another metal-rolling mill, as a builder's

labourer and back to the brickfields – all of which experiences he described most graphically in the memoirs he wrote half a century later. It was at this period of his young life that, when on strike, or because he had walked out, or for some other reason was unemployed, he learnt to box, to ride a three-wheel 'bone-shaker' and a penny-farthing bicycle. Then, in 1875, when he was eighteen, his mother remarried.

This was a clear case of hope triumphing over experience, for her second husband, a carpenter and joiner, was an even heavier drinker than her first and a man of violent temper into the bargain, so that Will seems to have found life intolerable at home and he left to take to the road as a casual labourer. At first he found work on the railway, which was hard and badly paid. Most of his wages went on board and lodging, though he did not fare too badly when it came to food, for he and his fellow navvies, with their lurcher dogs, went on poaching expeditions and he had his share of pheasants, partridges and rabbits.

He saved up enough to pay his fare back to Birmingham but, once there, he faced the unfamiliar problem of finding somewhere to live, not made easier by the fact that he could not get work for this was a period of severe trade depression.

When eventually he found a job it was seven

Coke barrow

miles distant from his lodgings. It entailed loading bricks on to canal barges and the long walk was more than he could face at each end of the day's heavy work. He took up his quarters with a quarrelsome, drunken old couple living on the canal in one of the narrowboats until he could stand their nightly brawling no more.

It was now, he claims, that he perceived that the reason unorganised labouring men put up with their appalling conditions was largely what he called their 'ignorance and boastfulness': they prided themselves upon being tough, going to the most extraordinary lengths to demonstrate their capacity to perform the heaviest tasks for the longest hours with no respite, as though this were in itself a merit, and without realising that it left them open to the most savage exploitation.

Once he was back in the city, Thorne joined his boyhood companions with whom he went in for pigeon-racing and also dog- and cock-fighting, which last two sports he thought disgustingly cruel. That winter he took a job at the Saltley gasworks as his father had done almost twenty years before. His task was to wheel into the yard the barrows of hot coke, then quenched with water, as it came from the retorts. 'Gruelling work' he called it, carried out for twelve-hour shifts, two weeks on days and two on nights, with the dreaded 'change-over' shift of 24 hours from a Sunday morning till the following day when 'every hour after the first twelve seemed like a month'.

As a minor and one of the last to have been taken on he was among the first to be dismissed when the retort houses closed down in the spring. He spent the next few months pleasantly enough in the open air helping one of his former bosses in the brickfields. But in the autumn he went back to the gasworks where he was shortly promoted to become a fully-fledged stoker.

This heavy, hot, hazardous task was performed, as were his previous jobs, in twelve-hour shifts, night and day, seven days a week. Its intensity had now been greatly increased by the introduction of a new type of furnace that saved as much as two hours' working time, carbonising four hundredweight of coal in as many hours – for it must be recalled that, until the 1960s, all gas was made from coal – but at a terrible cost to the men. In an inferno of badly-ventilated premises, filled with smoke and fumes, the temperature, even at a distance of ten feet from the retorts, reached 109° Fahrenheit. On a single charge men lost pounds of body weight, while the horrible burning of the retina of the eye often showed itself only years later in total blindness.

This was Thorne's first acquaintance with

Left: a lithograph of gas stokers by Gustav Doré. A good idea of hell; *above*, an 1890 ad man's representation of 'the Rapid Manual Apparatus'. A good idea of heaven.

the conditions that were to motivate his unique contribution to the character of British trade unionism, though it would be more than a decade before that promise was to be fulfilled. His immediate reaction was to try to get rid of the hated change-over shift by abolishing Sunday work altogether. He called a meeting of his fellow stokers and put the proposition to them. They did not believe it was practicable: if the retorts were allowed to cool down they would crack. Thorne argued that they seemed more concerned to safeguard the life-span of the retorts than their own. The men were at length persuaded it would be worth while a deputation approaching the resident engineer with Thorne as its spokesman. He was met, as might have been expected, by precisely the same objections as the men had voiced: it would shorten the life of the retorts to be left idle. However, it was conceded that the question should be put to the chief engineer – the equivalent of top management – who happened by ill chance to be a man of ungovernable temper which he now completely lost, threatening to sack all those on the deputation. Thorne parried this by saying that not only they but every man Jack in the works would then walk out. When he had calmed down the chief engineer agreed to put the matter to the owners, the Birmingham Corporation, who alone could decide upon it. This taught the men, who had been reluctant to challenge authority, that it paid to stick to their guns.

The upshot was that the Mayor of Birmingham himself, Joseph Chamberlain, visited the Saltley works with members of the Gas Committee before whom the proposition was formally laid within a fornight. It decided that Sunday work between the hours of 6 a.m. and 6 p.m. should be abolished, together with the 5 shillings for that day's work. This mixed blessing was shared by two other Corporation gasworks in the district.

From this, his first notable success as a leader at the age of twenty, Thorne drew the conclusion that without the combined backing of the workers, nothing could be won and he then and there tried to form a union, but failed. In after years he expressed the view that it was not only the men's backwardness and ignorance that prevented them from organising but that they simply

SCOOP-DRIVER.

lacked the courage. In making that harsh judgment – he went so far as to say that many workers were 'too cowardly to stand by their comrades in fighting for their rights' – Thorne perhaps gave too little weight to the men's legitimate dread of something even worse than ill-paid work in hideous conditions, namely, no work at all: victimisation, with its concomitants of blacklisting and the prospect of utter destitution. The masters never underestimated the deterrent effects of that fear, though sometimes they miscalculated.

To pay for that first victory Thorne was let off lightly though by no means scot-free. He was demoted for his audacity to the repulsive, dangerous and lower-paid work of 'purifier'.

It is strange to realise that this bold and intelligent young man was barely literate. Born thirteen years before the passing of the Elementary Education Act (by which elected boards could compel all parents to send their children between the ages of five and thirteen to school) Thorne was, of course, entirely self-taught; not to great effect in those early years it could be thought, for when at the age of 22 he married Harriet Hallam – the daughter of a man who followed the usual pattern of working in the brickfields in summer and at the gasworks in winter – neither he nor his bride could write their names.

No. 8 GAS-HOLDER.

To open the Inlet.—Go into the Governor House, at Shude Hill, and you will there see upon the floor four frames, with a handle upon each; the handle upon that frame which has the words "No. 8 Inlet" upon it, must be turned several times round in the opposite direction to that which the Sun takes; the handle must be turned round and round until it is ready for falling off. The Inlet will then be open, and the screw down.

To close the Inlet.—Turn the handle which is used for opening, in a contrary direction to that which you turn it for opening; that is, turn it the same way as the Sun goes. The handle must be turned round as often as you can, and the screw will be up when the Inlet is closed.

To open the Outlet.—Turn the handle which is upon the frame, with the words "No 8 Outlet" upon it, in a contrary direction to that which the Sun takes. Turn the handle round and round until you can turn it no longer, and the Outlet will be open.

To close the Outlet.—Turn the handle which is used for opening, in a contrary direction to that which you turn it for opening; that is, turn it round and round until you can turn it no longer, the same way as the Sun goes, and the Outlet will then be closed.

This undated document clearly refers to a period when such words as clockwise and anti-clockwise would not be understood, since a watch was a rare possession for working people before the 1860s.

The Air of Freedom

With the introduction of a new machine operating by compressed air, invented by John West and known as 'the iron man', conditions at Saltley gasworks worsened. Thanks to this machine the carbonising process was speeded up and the number of stokers on each gang reduced by half; but the new machine was constantly breaking down and had to be repaired. Thus where two men were now doing the work previously done by four, those two had never any time to eat, or rest, or take a breath of fresh air between charges. That situation became unendurable; men refused to go on; they took their pay and left.

Not long after that crisis, and despite the ties of a baby daughter and a pregnant wife, Thorne decided to try his luck in London on his own. This was in response to letters from a former workmate who sent glowing accounts of life in the capital. In November 1881 Thorne set out with two friends to walk the 120 miles to London with little in their pockets, occasionally sleeping rough and trusting to wayside generosity for food. Thorne at least had behind him not only the training of the long walks to and from work as a child but, at about sixteen, he had also taken up both walking and running as a sport, even accepting a challenge and winning a bet to run without a stop the eight miles between Birmingham and Coleshill.

Will Thorne at the age of 25

Drawing coke

Once the three young men reached London –
footsore and hungry – they made for the Old
Kent Road where Thorne's friend was employed
by the South Metropolitan Gas Company.
Thorne was taken on and put to his former job
as a wheeler. After a while he sent for his wife
and the baby and rented a small furnished
garret for 5 shillings a week where his second
daughter was born three months later. When
summer came and Thorne was no longer
needed at the gasworks the young family went
back to Birmingham where they stayed with
his parents-in-law. That winter he again
worked at Saltley, some seven miles away from
where he was now living but, to his dismay, the

stokers were confronted anew with the impossible task of manning the refractory 'iron man' that had caused so much trouble the year before. Again some of the men objected, but others were not prepared to support their protest nor the strike that Thorne now called. He saw the position as hopeless and left the works.

He then made the move that was to prove decisive for his future: he went to London once more, this time for good. Again he made the journey on foot with two companions and next to no money. He remembered a former Saltley workmate whom he succeeded in tracking down at the Beckton works of the Gas, Light & Coke company where all three travellers were given work. Once Thorne was settled in the job and had found two furnished rooms in Canning Town his wife and their now three children joined him. He was earning 5s 4d a day which, since he was trying to save money to furnish a home of his own and with five people to feed, did not go far in London. He made up his mind to become a teetotaller and signed the pledge. That was in 1885, by which time he was 28 and, it may be noted, no longer needed to put a cross in place of his signature.

In that year, as also in 1884, he had made active efforts to form a union at Beckton, succeeding up to a point only to see the fledgling organisations collapse after, in the one instance, a few weeks, in the other, a few months, owing to the men's fear of retribution. Certainly this was discouraging, but Thorne was far from giving up hope. He had joined the Social-Democratic Federation in 1884 and was one of the fourteen members of its Canning Town branch; he attended political lectures and even spoke on a public platform himself when he took the chair for Tom Mann, whom he now met for the first time. He also became acquainted with many of the notable figures in the socialist movement of the day and took a lively part in the great working-class demonstrations of that period, notably 'Black Monday' of 8 February 1886, when a somewhat unruly crowd, headed by John Burns carrying a red flag, marched through the West End of London causing alarm and despondency in clubland, and 'Bloody Sunday' of 13 November 1887, an occasion when huge numbers of the unemployed and their sympathisers, defying the Metropolitan Police ban on public meetings in Trafalgar Square, attempted to invade that precinct from every quarter and engaged in pitched battles with the police. By this time Thorne, in default of a gasworkers' union, had joined the small organisation of general labourers formed by his friend Ben Tillett.

Meanwhile at Beckton, where the work was harder and hotter, he recorded, than anything

Will Thorne, a portly figure on a soap box, addressing
members

he had known, he sedulously spread socialist propaganda, convinced that this would lead the men to understand the necessity to organise, while making sure that, by exemplary time-keeping and conscientious work, he gave his foreman no handle to victimise him. It was never far from his mind that the men would one day stand up and fight for decent conditions, when the company played into his hands by introducing at Beckton the troublesome 'iron man'. Owing to his experience of those machines, he was one of the first to be put to work on them. As at Saltley, the task was an impossible one: the heat, the perpetual breakdowns and the speed-up combined to produce strains which reached breaking point when the stokers were ordered on a Sunday to stay on to do an additional three charges, working until late into the night. That, as Thorne wrote, 'was the psychological moment for forming the union', and form it he did.

Although in later life, as Mayor of West Ham and a Member of Parliament, he became a thickset, even portly figure, a contemporary described him at this time as

> slight and fine-drawn through the heavy labour of his arduous calling. He came ... straight from the retort house with the mark of that fiery place burnt into his features. Round his eyes were dark rims of coal-grime, and his hands were ... gnarled and knotted by the handling of charging tools ...

It is extraordinary that, with such a childhood, youth and young manhood, Will Thorne, far from being brutalised or crushed, should have become ever more sensitively aware of the sufferings of his fellows, ever more conscious of and revolted by the degradation to which their masters debased them and ever more determined to battle against the causes of such suffering and degradation.

Ben Tillett

At Thorne's side on that sunny morning at the end of March in 1889 was 'the dear comrade and great fighter', Ben Tillett, a man of similar slight build, three years his junior, who had known an equally harsh childhood, though a more unhappy one for he had the misfortune to lose his mother when he was but a year old.

Born in September 1860 in John Street, Lower Easton, a few miles north-west of Bristol, Tillett, the youngest of the eight children of a worker in a comb factory, took little pleasure in recalling his early days. When he was over 70 years of age he wondered, looking back, whether he had ever had a childhood at all. While his older sisters and brothers went out into the world, he was left at the mercy of an ill-natured stepmother upon whose death she was almost at once replaced by another as unkind as the first, so that he was the defenceless prey to endless punishment and constant hunger. Twice as a very small child he ran away, only to be brought back to what was called his home.

At the age of six he became a wage earner. He was paid 1s 6d a week to cut clay for a brick moulder: toilsome work that, on fine days, started at five in the morning and went on until nightfall. Throughout his early boyhood he took to wandering the streets and, in particular, haunted the Bristol quays where he tried, unsuccessfully, to stow away in one of the ships moored there. From the seamen who discovered him and sent him packing he learnt the names of foreign countries, seas and ports. He took to frequenting the doss houses in the town where, in the evening, tramps and pedlars fore-gathered in the kitchens to cook and fight. They taught him boxing.

These meanderings were brought to an abrupt end when he adopted a terrier pup injured in a road accident – the first living creature, he wrote, to which he felt attached – and upon taking it back to his loveless home, he was told that neither he nor his new-found friend was welcome to stay there. In short, he was turned out. He took to the road, bent upon catching up with the circus which had come to town that winter when he had scraped an acquaintance with the owner's family. He knew that by now they would be well on their way to the Easter fairgrounds and so, nursing his pet, he followed their tracks, earning a few pence here and there by holding horses' reins, sleeping in the open and enquiring of other travellers – tramps and gypsies – where Old Joe Baker's circus might be found. He ran it to earth at last in Worcester: 50 miles from his starting point.

Like many a child before and since, little Tillett had fancied that circus life would be one long delight but swiftly discovered that, although warmly enough received by the family, he was expected to learn, and learn fast, the acrobatic tricks with which he must earn his keep. The exhausting practice sessions and performances, when every limb and muscle ached, were interspersed with the no less arduous business of packing up and helping to strike camp, followed by trekking through the night to pitch the tents anew and restart the cycle: a way of life made tolerable only by the genuine comradeship of the circus team.

It made its way in this manner through the Midlands until, somewhere near Stafford, out of the blue, one of Tillett's older sisters, now married, suddenly appeared to snatch him, as he put it, from the circus. He was just nine years old.

He had merely exchanged one form of drudgery for another, and this one of no interest at all, for he was obliged to give a hand with the domestic chores in his sister's large family. What was far worse, he was now sent to school. His formal education, however, was extremely short-lived. It appears that his teacher did not find him a rewarding pupil and made his dissatisfaction known by rapping him sharply on the knuckles with a heavy ruler so often that the boy, in a fury, resorting to modes of self-defence learnt in an altogether rougher school, used his fists, laying out his opponent unconscious on the floor. Although his sister bravely took up the cudgels on his behalf and threatened to sue the teacher for assault, Ben's reaction had been too unorthodox for the authorities of the National school to condone and he was expelled.

That was the end of his school life. For the next few years he took to the road again, picking up odd jobs and roaming about in search of adventure until, in 1873, at the age of thirteen, he found himself back in Bristol where his father agreed to sign the necessary papers for him to join the Royal Navy. This marked his final parting with his father and stepmother. He left them, he wrote, 'without regret and with only a perfunctory farewell'.

He joined his first ship in Plymouth where he

was kitted out. He referred to himself as a 'puny little thing', and it speaks volumes that there were no jackets or trousers, shoes or stockings small enough to fit him. Undersized he might be, but he withstood the rigours of the new, severe discipline of this hard life better than most. Not for nothing had he roughed it as 'a tired, penniless little tramp' in all weathers, while his young body had been hardened as an acrobat, 'racked to affect an unnatural contortion'.

The next two years he spent in a training ship lying in Falmouth Harbour during which time – in 1874 – the boys' weekly allowance was raised from 3d to 6d. He was then transferred for six weeks to learn practical seamanship aboard a sailing brig but, though he had done well in training, once he became an able-bodied seaman, posted to a battleship in the Channel fleet, he overreached himself by exercising what he called his 'old assertive passion for a race over the cross trees', winning a competition against all comers, but making one false move which landed him, seriously injured, in hospital. Upon his discharge he left the navy for good to join the merchant marine. In later years he recorded that:

> The holds I have worked in, and the docks I have trod, like the docks and wharfs I have tramped on, and the dockers and transport workers I have been associated with all my life, were my school and my school teachers.

Ben Tillett circa 1888

He enrolled in that school by sailing out of Bristol to cross the Atlantic in a full-rigged ship in the autumn of 1876, aged . sixteen. The homeward journey ended in the Pool of London and he found his way to Bethnal Green where another of his married sisters lived. There he was received with unexpected warmth so that it felt like a true home-coming such as he had never known. He was in fact more or less adopted in that household by his sister's mother-in-law and, in his turn, he adopted a young boy, ten years younger than himself, who lived with the family. In furthering the lad's education, Tillett, who claimed in after years that he had been illiterate at the age of fifteen, became a voracious reader.

Unable to find steady work in London he went back to Bristol where he signed on in a sugar trader's barque sailing to Barbados. Back in port he set off for London again and his newly-found home. He tried to join one of the two stevedores' trade unions at this time, but was not considered eligible. He took his place among the surging, struggling mass of men fighting like wild animals for an hour's or a half-hour's work on the docks for a few pence. It was here and then that young Tillett felt the first stirrings of rage against 'the horrible nightmare of the dockers' poverty' and 'the criminal wickedness of the exploitation that went on'.

The Air of Freedom

Alternating with casual work ashore, he went
to sea again. One of his last voyages was aboard
an old wooden 'Geordie' brig whose strong,
weatherbeaten skippers he much admired, and
in such a vessel he sailed to Riga. Having made
up his mind to go to sea no more he now made a
meagre living on the wharfs and in warehouses,
taking any job that came his way, whether on
the quays or in ships' holds, until he found more
regular work, first with the Nanking Tea
Company and then, on and off for some six or
seven years, as a cooper in the Monument Quay
warehouse at Swan Pier by London Bridge.

It was during this period that the most
formative events in his young life occurred.
While he continued the education of his little
protégé, vastly increasing his own knowledge in
the process, he married in 1882 a girl called
Jane Tomkins. He spoke of her as 'his brave
little wife', as well he might, for they lived in
two small back rooms in Bethnal Green where
their children were born, all but two of whom
died in infancy. To supplement the poor living
of a casual labourer Tillett mastered the craft of
shoemaking and joined the Boot and Shoe
Operatives' Union – established in 1874 – while
he agitated among the dockers, trying to rouse
them to protest against their inhuman
conditions.

It was almost by accident that he became

involved in founding a small trade union of general labourers in the East End of London. In July 1887, while employed in the Monument warehouse, he was approached by a friend working in a similar company in Cutler Street off Houndsditch which was threatening to reduce the wages of tea handlers. It emerged that other companies were planning to follow suit, that it was a concerted move, and the indignant workers called a meeting which Tillett was invited to attend. This marked the beginning of what he called 'properly my own life story'.

He went to the meeting in a pub off the Hackney Road without much hope that anything would come out of it. The men, aggrieved and excited, were quite unable to put forward any coherent proposals. A general air of anger and confusion reigned, goading Tillett, who saw clearly enough how they should proceed, into taking part. He had not intended to do anything of the kind, but he found himself hoisted up on to a table making a speech and listened to with close attention. He proposed that, for a start, a committee of twelve should be elected to draft the rules for a trade union. Thus the Tea Operatives' and General Labourers' Union – also known as the Tea Coopers' Association – came into being. It had no funds beyond the twopence a week contributions of its fluctuating

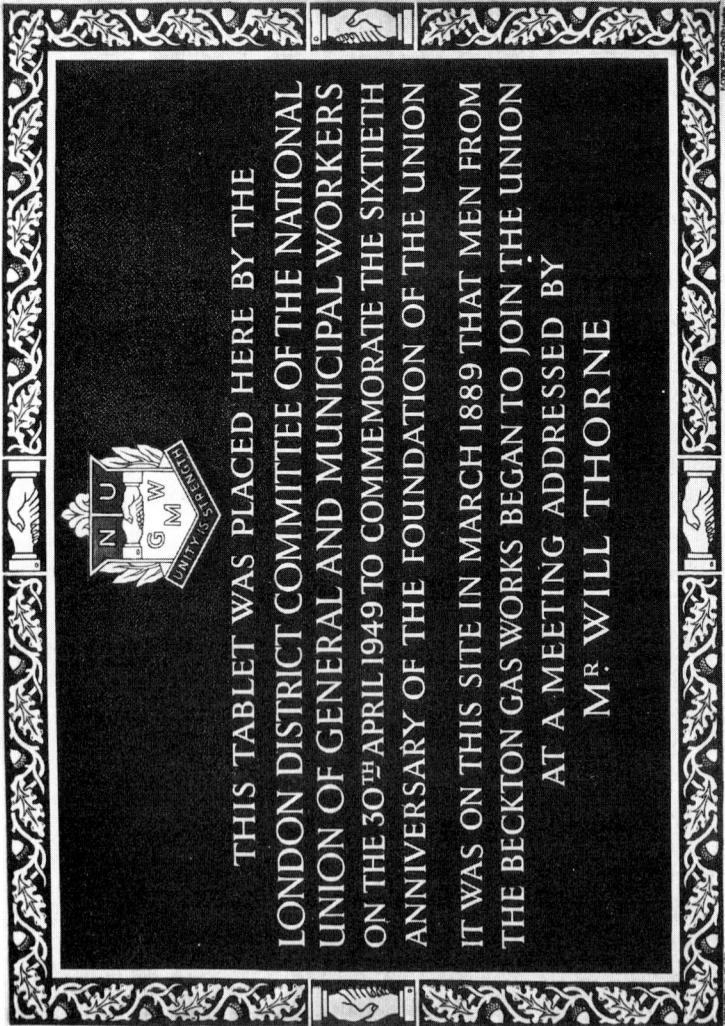

THIS TABLET WAS PLACED HERE BY THE
LONDON DISTRICT COMMITTEE OF THE NATIONAL
UNION OF GENERAL AND MUNICIPAL WORKERS
ON THE 30TH APRIL 1949 TO COMMEMORATE THE SIXTIETH
ANNIVERSARY OF THE FOUNDATION OF THE UNION

IT WAS ON THIS SITE IN MARCH 1889 THAT MEN FROM
THE BECKTON GAS WORKS BEGAN TO JOIN THE UNION
AT A MEETING ADDRESSED BY
MR. WILL THORNE

N U G W
UNITY IS STRENGTH

Plaque on the side of Canning Town Hall

membership of a few hundred men organised in three branches, with headquarters in a Poplar coffee house and its administration a somewhat nebulous affair that existed only in Tillett's own head.

As the General Secretary of this insecure, unimportant little organisation, appointed by his fellows at a wage of £2 a week, Tillett did not realise at first the profound change in his life that had been brought about by that first evening's work, for he was to retain the post of secretary for another 34 years: throughout his time as an alderman of the London County Council and as Labour MP for North Salford, long after his little union of 1887 had been merged into the Dock, Wharf, Riverside and General Workers' Union of Great Britain and Ireland, the forerunner of the mighty Transport and General Workers' Union of 1921, of which Tillett became the international and political secretary until 1930.

It was, however, as the moving spirit and secretary of an organisation of general workers, however insignificant in size, with many years' experience as a propagandist for trade unionism amongst the most downtrodden of casual labourers that Tillett was drawn by his friend Will Thorne into the events that brought about the founding of the Gasworkers' union in 1889.

At a preliminary meeting held in the Barking

Canning Town Hall stands on the site of the founding
meeting 31 March 1889

Road on 24 March with Thorne in the Chair and
Tillett among the speakers, it was decided in
principle to form a union. The 800 men present
at that meeting readily paid their 1 shilling
entrance fee and it was agreed that a
deputation of eight stokers – four men from
each shift – should go to the Beckton manager
to put the case for an eight-hour day.

The famous 'birthday' meeting on the
following Sunday morning, 31 March, was
attended by 2,500. 'The atmosphere was
electric,' when, as Thorne wrote, he mounted
the old van that served as a platform. His
speech stuck closely to the point: here among
his audience were those who had just come off
an eighteen-hour stint:

> Let me tell you that you will never get any alteration in
> Sunday work, no alteration in any of your conditions or
> wages, unless you join all together to form a strong trade
> union ... Stand together this time ... This morning I want
> you to swear and declare that you mean business and
> that nothing will deter you from your aim ... The way you
> have been treated at your work for many years is scanda-
> lous, brutal and inhuman. I pledge my word that, if you
> will stand firm and don't waver, within six months we
> will claim and win the eight-hour day, a six-day week
> and the abolition of the present slave-driving methods in
> vogue not only at the Beckton Gas Works but all over the
> country ...

After Thorne had spoken, Tillett addressed the
crowd in moving terms, describing his unsuc-
cessful efforts to organise the dockworkers

whose appalling working conditions cried out for redress. Their time would come, he predicted and, in the meanwhile, he was happy to be present at this heartening occasion.

A provisional committee, consisting of Thorne, Tillett and William Byford was formed and, as soon as the meeting was over, sat down to draft a preliminary set of rules, including a proposed membership contribution of 2d a week. That draft was put to a delegate meeting for endorsement and it was then moved that the new union should put forward to all the London gas companies a claim for a wage rise of 1 shilling a day. That, of course, would have been the most natural move, but it was strongly opposed by Thorne who said that they should abide by the single and most important point if they wanted to succeed: the question of the eight-hour shift was paramount and could only be weakened if other demands were advanced at the same time.

It was a mark of the maturity of the delegates that his view won the day. Thus the single issue of shorter working hours became the cause upon which the new union took its stand.

A petition was then presented to the gas companies and, after a slightly anxious period of waiting for a response, the Gas, Light & Coke company at Beckton – by far the largest of the undertakings – conceded the eight-hour day: that is, there were to be three shifts in the 24 hours instead of two, without any reduction of wages. This was to apply to the company's other gasworks in the metropolis. Thorne later wrote that:

> It was a milestone in Trade Union history and one of the greatest victories ever achieved ... Our Union put heart into thousands of unskilled, badly paid and unorganised workers ...

At the delegate meeting, held in May, both Thorne and Tillett were nominated for the position of General Secretary. Both had reservations about accepting the office: Thorne because he thought he was too ill-educated, Tillett because he felt that his first loyalty was to the dockers. He saw it as his primary duty to rouse those cowed and intimidated men from their apathy and foresaw that weeks if not months of unstinting – and probably heart-breaking – effort would be needed to organise them.

In this he was not mistaken, for the great conflagration of the Dock Strike – sparked off, there can be no doubt, by the torch lit by the gasworkers in forming the first viable union of labouring men – was to break out only three months later: in August 1889. Tillett was therefore in no way aggrieved when the result of the ballot for the General Secretaryship of the gasworkers, announced in June, gave Thorne an overwhelming majority of over 2,000

Shifting coke

votes. His salary was £2 5s a week.

In the three months past a great recruiting drive had taken place. Each Sunday as many as twenty horse-drawn wagonloads of men would start out from the union headquarters in the Barking Road to call on other gasworks. In the first two weeks 3,000 had joined the union and throughout April and May speakers, often led by a brass band, visited King's Cross, Vauxhall, Battersea, Nine Elms, Fulham, Kensal Green, Deptford and the Old Kent Road, everywhere making new members.

By the time the First Half-Yearly Report and Balance Sheet for the period 31 March to 30 September was presented there were 43 metropolitan branches, including two with over 1,000 members, and nineteen in the provinces. On this occasion Thorne felt obliged to apologise for the shortcomings of the balance-sheet: he had spent two nights without sleep and many days working on it among a confusion of scraps of paper, some of which were indecipherable. Not only was he himself quite unaccustomed to clerical work, but many of the branch secretaries with the best will in the world were so inexperienced in book-keeping and paperwork in general that they were as yet not able to produce legible accounts. This, however, in his view, time and practice would correct and was not in any case at that stage of the union's existence of paramount importance. As he said in his address:

> ... some time since, what were your conditions, twelve long hours per day without cessation and this continued for weeks together, no time for recreation, no time to visit your friends ... and the whole of this time hastening to premature death, to leave your wives and children to become paupers ... Now you are working the eight-hour day ... I challenge any workmen to show where any of the working classes demonstrated in the same manner as the gas stokers. We are at present one of the strongest Labour unions in England. It is true that we have only one benefit attached and that is strike pay ... the whole aim and intention of the Union is to reduce the hours of labour ...

The social benefits of the shorter hours of work, which Thorne emphasised again and again, were strikingly illustrated in a conversation quoted by Sydney Webb in a pamphlet he wrote with Harold Cox in 1891:

> When the gas stokers of Beckton ... won the Eight Hour Day in 1889, it was noted by their Trade Union Secretary that several of them took out of pawn the black cloth coats in which they had been married, but which they had not, with the Twelve Hour Day, had much opportunity to wear.

To reach the conviction that unskilled workers, in general despised and thought to be – if they did not consider themselves – incapable of organising, should and could form unions, Thorne and Tillett had travelled the roughest road, by way of the exploitation of child labour, casual and seasonal employment under bullying foremen and despotic masters, and the vile working conditions that prevailed in the brickfields, gasworks, docks and ware-houses: wherever, indeed, general labourers in the late nineteenth century were employed. Neither of them, of course, had much facility as orators, Thorne being an entirely unpractised and somewhat tongue-tied speaker with a poor voice, while Tillett was handicapped by a stammer. In time both of them learnt to conquer their weaknesses and acquitted themselves in this respect, as in the administrative sphere, with great credit.

John Burns

Unfamiliar with trade union methods and practice, Thorne and Tillett leant gratefully upon the help offered by such men as John Burns and Tom Mann, skilled workers and members of the powerful Amalgamated Society of Engineers, established in 1851. These two gave their unstinted support to the new union because they were, in fact, wholly out of sympathy with the attitude of the permanent officials of their own and other craft, so-called 'New Model' unions to whom the Webbs had given the collective name of 'the Junta' – Engineers, Ironfounders, Carpenters and Joiners and suchlike – an

TO THE
GASWORKERS OF LEEDS!

ON SUNDAY NEXT

Sept. 15th. 1889,

A MASS

MEETING

of Gasworkers & General Labourers,

Will be held in

VICARS CROFT.

AT 3 O'CLOCK P.M. PROMPT.

MR G. THORNE

Sec.; of the National Union of

GASWORKERS & GENERAL LABOURERS,

and others will address the meeting.

:o:

A SECOND MEETING

Will be held in the evening at 7, o'clock, p.m. at the

Meeting-Rooms, of the

→* SOCIALIST LEAGUE. *←

Clarendon Buildings, Victoria Road,

GASWORKERS & OTHERS SHOULD MAKE A
point of attending both these Meetings.

Leeds gasworkers' 1889 recruitment leaflet.
Even in those days printers made mistakes!

URGENT TO ALL MEMBERS.

No. 1 BRANCH BRISTOL GAS WORKERS

You are summoned to attend

MEETINGS

To be held at

NEW STREET BRITISH WORKMAN,

ST. JUDE'S, ON

Monday Morning, at 10 a.m.,

And also in

Evening, at 6.30 p.m., on March 7th, 1892,

TO TAKE INTO CONSIDERATION

The New Scheme of Messrs. DIX, FIDDES, and IRVING.

Hoping the whole of the Members will attend.

By order of the Management Committee,

JAMES VICKERY, *Chairman.*

FREDK. TOWNSEND, *Secretary.*

Jenkins, Printer and Stationer, Rupert Street, Bristol.

Activity in the provinces: Bristol gasworkers
meeting 1892

attitude described by a contemporary as:

> the cautious, the thrifty, contented, rest-and-be-thankful temper of a bank director or a City magnate.

John Burns himself wrote:

> Their reckless assumption of the duties and responsibilities that only the State or the whole community can discharge in the nature of sick and superannuation benefits ... is crushing out the larger unions by taxing their members to an unbearable extent ... the fear of being unable to discharge their friendly society liabilities often makes them submit to encroachments by the masters without protest. The result is that all of them have ceased to be unions for maintaining the rights of labour and have degenerated into mere middle and upper-class rate-reducing institutions ...

Clearly Burns felt more in tune with the spirit and objectives of the Gasworkers' union which offered one and only one benefit to its members, namely, strike pay. He flung himself readily into taking part – and a leading part – in its recruiting campaign.

John Burns was born in October 1858 in South Lambeth, the sixteenth of eighteen children and the second son of Alexander Burns, an engine-fitter from Ayrshire who had moved south in the 1850s with his wife Barbara who came from Aberdeen. Nine of the children survived and John certainly knew poverty, though not want. Neither, though presumably somewhat overcrowded, was the home an unhappy one, despite the fact that, contrary to John's own later version of events, his father, who died in 1876 when John was eighteen, appears to have deserted his enormous family much earlier, leaving the mother to fend for her brood of living – and dying – children. She seems to have managed this well enough, though quite illiterate, having signed John's birth certificate with a cross.

He went to school until he was ten: first in Lambeth and then, after the family moved, in Battersea. After that he had odd jobs as a page-boy in a private house and helper in both a pub and a bakery before he was twelve, at which time he became employed full-time for two years by Price's Patent Candle Company in Battersea Park Road, earning 4 shillings a week for some 60 hours' work. He next went as a riveter to an engineering firm in Wandsworth; but by then had saved enough money to pay for his own apprenticeship in engineering. Twice, for reasons not known but thought to be his unwillingness to truckle to authority, his indentures were cancelled, but he came out of his time at Mowlem's, one of the largest contractors, at the usual age.

In 1874, now 21, he went to West Africa for a couple of years, engaged by the Royal Niger Company as a foreman engineer despite his youth. Shortly after his return to England he married Martha Charlotte Gale – a girl he had met before he went away – by whom he had one son.

He rose to public prominence in the years when the demonstrations by the unemployed were at their height by being arrested in February 1886 on the occasion of the riots on 'Black Monday'. The part he had played then and his fiery speech from the dock earned him the title of 'The Man with the Red Flag' – reprinted as a pamphlet of that name – and also his acquittal. However, on 'Bloody Sunday' – 13 November 1887 – he was again arrested, and this time sentenced to six weeks in jail for his part in the battles with the police in Trafalgar Square.

Although his schooling had been brief and sketchy, he had educated himself by wide reading and had become an eloquent and rousing speaker whose splendid stentorian voice was always at the service of the workless, of free speech and of the Social-Democratic Federation which he joined in August 1884. Later that year, when others were splitting off, at odds with the leadership, Burns not only stayed, a staunch supporter of Hyndman, but became a member of his Executive, only to quarrel with him eventually in 1889, when he resigned from the Federation and formed the Battersea Labour League.

John Burns, 1886

It was this little group that nominated him as the Socialist candidate for the newly formed London County Council that year, and it was thanks to his tremendous local popularity that he was returned top of the poll. His supporters set up a John Burns Fund to provide him with a salary of two guineas a week so that he could devote himself to his local government and general political duties.

The year 1889, marked by that triumph and by the outstanding successes of the Gas-workers' Union and the Dock Strike, in both of which Burns had played a spectacular part in heading processions and speaking everywhere, was the apogee of his career as a leader of the working class. Although he kept a diary on and off for most of his adult life – donated to the British Library after his death in 1943 – there are, unfortunately, no entries for that significant year.

The final rupture with his socialist friends came four years later when a second Battersea seat on the LCC fell vacant and, though a Labour candidate stood, John Burns supported the Liberal, who won. It is ironical that he, who of all those with whom he stood shoulder to shoulder in the heady days of 1889, was to end his active political life as a pillar of the Liberal establishment – President of the Board of Trade and a Cabinet Minister in the Asquith government – should have taken the most extreme view at the time, vehemently opposing the demand for the shorter working day on the grounds, according to Tom Mann's account of the occasion,

> … that the time had passed for such trivial reforms as the eight-hour day. Amid loud cheers he declared that the capitalist system was on its last legs and that it was our duty to prepare at once to seize the whole of the means of production and wipe out the capitalists altogether …

That was in 1886, at a meeting of the local SDF branch, of which Burns and Mann were at that time fellow members, as they were also of the ASE: Burns in the West London and Mann in the Battersea branch.

Because the union branch gave no scope for the discussion of general topics, Mann and a few others formed the Battersea Progressive Society, to 'shake up the Engineers', as he put it, the union having become, in his opinion, 'very respectable and very dull'.

Tom Mann

Burns and Mann were at this period good friends, despite their great difference on the eight-hour day, which Burns could brush aside as mere tinkering with an irrelevant issue instead concentrating upon the swift overthrow of the capitalist system, while Mann was a tireless and committed advocate for this immediate reform. Since it was not a question that engaged the attention of the Battersea branch of the SDF, Mann called his Progressive Society together in April 1886 and, after a lengthy debate, a vote was taken in favour of setting up a committee of fifteen to launch an Eight Hours League. Several branches of that organisation were formed in London and a few elsewhere, while its adherents met regularly and the League offered speakers to any trade union branch. This was taken up eagerly and proved so effective that, at a specially convened conference of trade unionists held in Southwark, over 80 per cent of the delegates voted for the introduction of the legal eight-hour day.

It was following this that, in June 1886, Mann published his influential pamphlet *What the Compulsory Eight Hour Day Means to the Workers* in which he wrote:

> I cannot understand a workman who through youth and early manhood has been battling against long hours in order that he might attend the institute, listen to the lectures and read the works of able men, and by these means has succeeded in having a mind worth owning – I say I cannot understand such a one hindering rather than helping in a shorter hours' movement. He practically says by the leisure he used so well as to become a man thereby, others will use so ill that they will continue fools ...

Whether that was intended as a sly rebuke to

Burns cannot be known. Mann's strongest argument, however, concerned the central matter of unemployment:

> What ... can be more rational than to ease the burden of those in work and the starving stomachs of those who are out by shortening the working day?

He developed this theme in well-documented and persuasive terms and there can be no doubt that Thorne, toiling away for twelve hours by day or by night in the Beckton retort house, was among Mann's many readers.

As early as 1885 Mann had addressed the young Fabian Society – which then numbered 40 members – on this subject and, although he did not appear to realise that such a demand had been afoot as long ago as in the 1830s and again in the '60s, he was extremely well-informed on the recent history of the eight-hour day movement.

His special importance to the formation of the Gasworkers' Union lay precisely in the fact that he had for so long been in the forefront of this movement. When he addressed the mass meeting of gasworkers held to celebrate their victory in July 1889, he declared:

> They had won mainly because they had a one-plank platform. Had they gone for half-a-dozen reforms they might have been agitating vainly for years without accomplishing anything tangible. As it was they had fought a pitched battle on the eight-hour day and in

fifteen weeks had won a victory that put older and larger trade unions to shame.

A further celebration was held not long after – on 28 July – when 12,000 people marched from the Embankment to Hyde Park. In the same month Mann's second pamphlet, *The Eight Hours Movement*, written in May, was published. In this he cited the progress of the movement in eight Continental countries and also in Australia, where the demand was being widely popularised.

Nor did he fail to point out that it was the United States that had really made the running. It was a fact, not to be overlooked, that the American Federation of Labour at its Annual Convention in December 1888 held in St Louis had decided to call mass meetings in every city to discuss the eight-hour day on four designated dates: 4 July 1889 (Independence Day), 2 September (Labour Day), 2 February 1890 (Washington's birthday), to culminate in a mass demonstration on 1 May. This last date was endorsed by the International Socialist Labour Congress held in Paris in July 1889, attended by over 400 delegates from 22 countries, who voted that:

> a great manifestation on a fixed date, simultaneously in all countries and in all towns, on the same agreed day the workers will call upon the public authorities to reduce the working day by law to eight hours.

(It may be said in parenthesis that the A.F. of L. resolution was itself the outcome of earlier agitation in support of a shorter working day. At the 1884 Convention of the Federation of Organized Trades and Labour Unions – the forerunner of the A.F. of L. – it was proposed that May the First 1888 should be proclaimed a nationwide strike to enforce the eight-hour day. The 1885 Convention ratified this decision and, when the date arrived, some 300,000 workers from over 11,000 enterprises took to the streets and paraded in Chicago, Detroit, New York and other industrial centres, winning the eight-hour day for more than 20,000 workers.)

Tom Mann's new pamphlet pointed out that all the arguments deployed in the past by opponents of the Ten Hours Act and the Nine Hours Movement had been proved false. He drew various examples from the engineering industry and also dwelt upon the effect that legislation to reduce hours of work would have on the 'sweating dens' whose exploited home-workers would no longer be without any alternative: once labour was in greater demand, they would be able to exercise the choice of working in a factory for a stated time compared with which nobody in their senses, unless forced by very special circumstances, would opt for doing underpaid work for limitless hours.

Mann's own interest in the subject dated back to 1871 when he was a fifteen-year-old in his second year of apprenticeship at Thomas Chatwin's Victoria Works in Birmingham making hand-tools for engineers and gas fitters. There he worked the statutory 60-hour week – from 6 a.m. till 6 p.m. on five days and from 6 a.m. till 3 p.m. on Saturdays, with two extra, unpaid, hours – when, as a result of an eighteen-week strike by Tyneside engineers, a nine-hour working day was won for the entire engineering industry and a number of other trades. This came into force in January 1872.

Mann's apprenticeship was begun in the year that saw the passing of the Elementary Education Act when it dawned upon him, as he wrote in later life, that he had missed something of enormous importance: other boys could now go to school all day until they were twelve or thirteen, whereas he had been at work since the age of nine.

Born in April 1856 in Bell Green, Foleshill, a suburb two-and-a-half miles to the north-east of Coventry, Tom was the third child and the second son of Thomas Mann, the clerk to the Victoria colliery, and his wife Ann who died when Tom was two years old. The father's second wife, whom he married five years later, was an amiable woman and a kindly step-

mother so that, unlike Will Thorne or Ben
Tillett, Tom Mann enjoyed a happy and secure
childhood, experiencing neither poverty nor
neglect.

After a year of doing what he called:

> odd jobs in the fields: bird-scaring, leading the horses
> at the plough, stone-picking, harvesting and so on,

he was allowed by law once he had reached the
age of ten, to go down the pit which employed
his father. His task was to crawl on hands and
feet in pitch darkness dragging a sledge-like
box of coal attached by a chain and belt to his
waist. The appalling strain of this work was
such that in late life he could recall groaning
aloud in agony, particularly when the rough
surface of the track was wet and slippery. He
plied this dreadful trade for four whole years,
until 1870. (He was unlucky, for only a couple of
years later, with the passing of the Mines
Regulation Act, no humans, let alone small
boys, were permitted to do such work. Even the
horses who replaced them drew the load on
rails and along wider, better-lit underground
passages than those in which lads like Tom
Mann had dragged their painful way.)

By then, however, a serious fire had broken
out in the Victoria mine. It proved to be
inextinguishable and the colliery was closed.
The family, with everyone else dependent upon

Tom Mann, 1889

it for work, moved away and the Manns settled in Birmingham where Tom began his apprenticeship.

Of a serious turn of mind and religiously inclined, Tom became a regular Sunday School pupil and churchgoer. Once the nine-hour day was instituted and overtime banned, he found other opportunities to study, attending an evening institute three times a week, as well as Bible classes and meetings of the temperance society which he now joined. He learnt about machine construction and design, while from a Quaker who taught in one of his scripture classes he took lessons in the correct use of his native tongue, elocution, etymology and a true respect for the English language.

Although he listened to lectures by such secularists and non-religious freethinkers as Bradlaugh, Foote and Annie Besant, he took no interest in economics or politics at this time and was certainly no socialist, for the revival of that movement was still to come, while trade unionism – dominated at that time by 'the Junta' of the craft union leaders – meant little or nothing to him since it called for no activity among the members.

By the time Mann reached the end of his apprenticeship at the age of 21 he was well read – having used to good advantage the Birmingham Public Library – and self-educated in a wide variety of subjects, though single-minded in his Christian, almost missionary zeal. He went to London where, owing to the recession in the engineering industry at that point in 1877, he could find no work and eventually took a job as a clerk at Swan and Edgar's department store in Piccadilly Circus. It was not long, however, before he got his first employment as a fully qualified tradesman with the Westinghouse Brake Company in King's Cross.

His main interests at this stage of his life, apart from his religion, were food reform – he became a vegetarian for some years – astronomy and a dawning preoccupation with such social questions as the failure of charitable agencies to allay what he described as 'the totality of misery, or to minimise the sum of human suffering'.

Various engineering jobs followed and it was while he was working at Thorneycroft's in Chiswick, which produced torpedo blades, that he came upon and was deeply impressed by Henry George's *Progress and Poverty*, first published in 1879. He declared this book 'by far the most valuable' he had ever read. At the same period he was greatly influenced by an eccentric workmate, a Scotsman, who had a passion for Shakespeare with which he infected Tom Mann for life.

In 1882 he made his first trip abroad, going to

Paris for a week, while in the following year he sailed for New York where he worked for four months in the engineering department of a Brooklyn sugar refinery. On his return to London, while employed by a series of different engineering firms, he attended classes on science and art. He also started and became the President of a Shakespeare Mutual Improvement Society, whose serious nature is well illustrated by the syllabus for the first half-year for the year 1884. It included such diverse subjects as the Nature of Electricity, the Chemistry of the Sun, the Circulation of the Blood, the Tower of London and – a leap in the dark – Are Other Worlds Inhabitable? Mann himself lectured on both Henry George and astronomy, while the members spent their free Saturday afternoons visiting museums. These earnest pursuits, beyond demonstrating a hunger for learning, did not appear to lead anywhere in particular until at the age of 28 Mann got hold of Thorold Rogers' *Six Centuries of Work and Wages*, published in 1884, which had so great an effect upon him as to determine the future course of his life.

Not until then, he himself recorded, had he acquired the slightest grasp of social economics, but now, almost immediately, he became convinced of the real necessity to reduce the hours of labour: a matter in which, so far as he knew, no one was showing the smallest interest, though it was a moment that coincided with the rapid growth of the Social-Democratic Federation whose Battersea branch Tom, now living in that area, joined in the spring of 1885. No sooner had he done so than he threw himself heart and soul into its activities. He was immensely impressed by the forthright and fearless way that his friend and fellow-engineer John Burns and others presented the case for socialism and what he called 'the amount of valuable information they imparted'. He was determined to become equally effective and worked hard at it, devoting every weekend to propaganda work and

> usually speaking three times on the Sunday: twice in
> the open air and once indoors,

a considerable change from the pious Sundays of his earlier days, though he himself recognised that he was bringing to this new ideology 'the old religious fervour' of his past, even to the point of risking dismissal from his job in one company after another.

Indeed, by early in 1887 he was so notorious as a socialist proselytiser that he could not get work anywhere. So began his full-time activity for the SDF which assigned to him the task of going to Newcastle upon Tyne during a strike of the Northumberland miners to report on the prospects of initiating a programme of socialist education in the county. He not only reported but started the work and carried it on for a whole year, during which he also went to Dundee to give a series of lectures. At the end of the year he took a factory job in Wallsend but was sacked after four days when his name was brought to the employer's notice. The same thing happened at the next job a week later and he realised that he had been blacklisted throughout the country – certainly in his own trade – and found himself obliged to part with his most treasured possessions – his books, his telescope and his violin – in order to live.

He was not sorry to be asked to do another stint for the SDF by going to Bolton and, when the people there pressed him to stay on as the Lancashire organiser, he readily agreed. He gave lectures on economics and spoke regularly in the Town Hall square.

A contemporary witness wrote that he:

> drew very large crowds … his fiery speeches were marvels of eloquence and power … The Authorities got alarmed with the results of his brilliant, burning eloquence and his name was taken by the police authorities with a view to prosecution for creating an obstruction … Tom stoutly stood to his guns, he never flinched, the crowds grew to enormous dimensions, his popularity increased … he was one of the best speakers I have known … with the first word uttered, he gripped his audience and kept them spellbound until the end …

Charging a retort

It was but a few weeks after his return to London in 1889 that he was made aware of the agitation among the Beckton gasworkers for an eight-hour day. In company with Burns he met Will Thorne, was immediately involved, and pressed the point that before making any formal demand to the company the men must first be organised. Thus it was that Tom Mann was in at the very start of the movement to form the Gasworkers' Union. Both he and Burns offered to help in any way they could and were as good as their word, addressing, each in his own practised and powerful style, the vast recruiting meetings held every Sunday that spring outside the premises of all the London gasworks until, as Mann wrote, 'in a few weeks 90 per cent of the men were organised.'

It was now and in the course of this activity that Mann first met Ben Tillett and was thus, in due course, drawn into taking a leading part in the Dock Strike a few months later, to become the first president of the Dock, Wharf, Riverside Workers and General Labourers' Union established after and as a result of the strike, with branches in every port. He retained that position for four years (1889-92) and thereafter, until 1903, was the honorary president.

Eleanor Marx

The fifth person to be closely associated with the birth and early days of the Gasworkers' Union was not a worker and not even a man, but a middle-class female: Eleanor Marx, the youngest daughter of Karl Marx who had died six years earlier bequeathing to that daughter much of his revolutionary vision, a very clear understanding of socialist theory and a firm belief in internationalism, expressed in the phrase 'Workers of all lands, unite!'

Born in January 1855 in Dean Street, Soho, in the West End of London and brought up in Grafton Terrace, Kentish Town, in what is now the Borough of Camden and was then St

Eleanor Marx circa 1890

Pancras, Eleanor Marx did not owe so much to the education she irregularly received at a little private school for young ladies in Haverstock Hill – where the fees were as irregularly paid, for the Marxes were always in debt – as to an exceptionally learned home environment where books were regarded as not less – if not more – essential than food. Since early childhood she had listened to and, being precocious, even taken part in highly political conversations and as she grew up in that household she absorbed and adopted as perfectly natural the most advanced political and social ideas from which she never deviated.

Although as a young woman she had entertained high ambitions to go on the stage, these were disappointed, but her training as an actress stood her in good stead as a public speaker with a beautiful voice and a total lack of self-consciousness. By 1889, when she was 34, she already knew Will Thorne fairly well. She it was who, in his own words,

> helped me more than anyone else to improve my very bad handwriting, my reading and general knowledge.

Her influence on Thorne personally and on the whole early development of the union was pervasive and incalculable. To her was owed not only the broad internationalist element that gave the young union such a high standing

Biscuit workers male and female were among the first
to join the Gas Workers and General Labourers Union.

with its older Continental brethren, but it was Eleanor Marx who introduced – one could say inspired – a sane and respectful attitude to women as trade unionists when that was rare indeed.

At the time she first came upon the scene of the gasworkers she had been living openly for the past five years with Edward Aveling, a man who, according to Bernard Shaw,

> would have gone to the stake for Socialism and atheism, but with absolutely no conscience in his private life.

They were not married because Aveling had a wife from whom he was separated but Eleanor, elected to the Executive of the Gasworkers' Union, was known throughout the trade union movement as 'Sister Aveling'.

She was no honorary member but a most active one, not only as a speaker but as the secretary of the first women's branch of the Gasworkers, which she had formed in October 1889, and in helping to form a number of other branches. She was greatly in demand to address meetings in all parts of the country. Her political judgment and sound common-sense were invaluable, not only to Thorne but to the whole organisation. She had no delusions about the imminent overthrow of British capitalism but a strongly rooted faith in the action of ordinary working men and women, united in national and international solidarity, to bring about progress towards a more humane and equitable society.

In a backroom capacity she helped to draw up the Gasworkers' provisional rules which were to be debated and endorsed – or revised – at the first Annual Conference held at Whitsun 1890 in the Workmen's Club in Gye Street, Kennington, attended by some 67 delegates. She was also responsible for drafting Thorne's Conference address, in which he said:

> The immediate objects of this Union are the improvement of the material conditions of its members; the raising them from mere beasts of burden to human beings; the saving of little children from the hard, degrading, bitter life to which they are condemned today; the dividing more equally between all men and women the tears and laughter, the sorrow and joy, the labour and leisure of the world ...

The sentiments are, unmistakably, Will Thorne's, but the words are those of Eleanor Marx.

At this Conference her every intervention was listened to with respect and her proposals were readily accepted by the delegates. It is noteworthy that, under Rule 2, which defined the union's objects, there was a clause stating that one of these was to 'obtain for the same work the same wages for women as for men'.

This item was proposed by a man and seconded by a woman delegate, while a rider to that rule stated firmly that:

> whenever in these Rules the word 'man', 'him', or 'his' occur, they shall be taken to mean 'man or woman', 'he or she', 'his or her', 'him or her'. Our Union is of men and women and our Rules apply to both.

In the prolonged debate on the investment of funds – Rule 9 – one of the Bristol delegates moved that there should be no investment in any company paying dividends, saying:

> We do not believe in interest. We all have to suffer under this damnable interest-mongering. We object to sweating and can therefore not profit by the sweating companies. At the present time I know we must make a compromise and must invest somewhere. I propose we invest only in Government and Municipal Securities – not that we are ignorant of the fact that the Government today is also a sweater ...

This provoked a lively discussion, some delegates being of the view that it would be wholly idiotic to settle for a return of 2 or 3 per cent when the funds could be earning 10 or 12 per cent. The matter was finally clinched by Pete Curran, a Scotsman employed at Woolwich Arsenal and here representing the Plumstead branch, though at this Conference he was elected to the Executive and would shortly become the union's most effective organiser. He argued that:

Pete Curran in his middle years. Curran was a full-time officer of the union from 1889 to 1910.

Laundry workers. Detail of the Gas Workers' emblem

> The first of all principles is to practice what you preach.
> If we denounce ... paying large dividends by means of
> sweating, it would be absurd and inconsistent to go and
> invest in the companies we denounce ...

The opposition amendment was defeated and
the Rule laid down, as originally drafted, that
no investment should be made in 'any Deben-
tures or any Security of any Company paying a
Dividend'.

When it came to the election of officers,
William Byford – who was a former secretary of
the Yorkshire Glassblowers' Association, and
would become Thorne's father-in-law upon his
second marriage in 1894 – was persuaded,
rather against his will, to continue as
Treasurer: a position he had occupied from the
start. Thorne was unanimously re-elected as
General Secretary, with a weekly salary now
raised to £2 10s and it was agreed that the
Executive should consist of fifteen members,
eight of whom were to be from north and seven
from south of the Thames.

It says much for Sister Aveling's standing
that she was the sole nominee to be elected not
only unanimously but by acclaim, so that her
name had not even to be put to the vote. She
was also one of the nine delegates chosen to go
to the Liverpool TUC to be held in September
1890: the first occasion of the Gasworkers'
affiliation to that body.

Brickmaking in the 1940s. The process of handmaking bricks has hardly changed since Thorne and his family worked in the brickfields more than half a century earlier.

When the time came, those delegates represented 60,000 members, the majority of whom – some 30,000 – were gasworkers, with the next largest number being employed in Yorkshire dyeworks; but some 70 other occupations were also represented in such diverse industries as chemicals, breweries, laundries, brick-making, confectionery, jute, sugar and so on: it was in truth, from the start a *trades* union rather than a trade union; and by the end of that year 1890 it had separate district organisations in Belfast, Birkenhead, Birmingham, Bristol, Dublin, Manchester, Plymouth and Sunderland, each including members in a great variety of occupations.

If Eleanor Marx's influence upon the union was vital, this was a two-way effect. Her dealings with and for the gasworkers provided an ever-expanding acquaintance with masses of working men and women: an irreplaceable experience, so that when, largely owing to personal circumstances, she resigned from the union's Executive in June 1895, she severed one of her most valuable life-lines. In a single stroke it cut off the reciprocal flow of learning and teaching, as well as the mutual admiration and affection that characterised her relations with both the leaders and the members of the union. There can be no doubt that this loss of so valuable a stimulus sapped her vitality, to play some part in whatever it was that led to the final discouragement and despair manifested by her suicide in 1895 at the age of 43.

II

The Opposition

The common bond uniting the founders of the union, apart from personal friendship, was their socialism.

For those living in the 1980s under the low-lying pall of Thatcherism, where the highest human aspiration is supposed to be the ownership of shares on the stock market, it is hard to realise how exhilarating were the socialist principles that inspired Thorne and his fellows, not only in awakening a spirit of hope – and of endeavour to realise that hope – but in greatly expanding the horizons of men and women whose circumstances had narrowed their outlook.

Socialism in the Britain of the 1880s, dormant since the demise of the Chartist movement a generation earlier, was revived in a wholly different society: one in which the new methods of production, the modern forms of transport on land and sea and of public utilities

Women rubber workers joined the union in 1890, Dunlop's Ltd, Birmingham

affected every sphere of life for both producers and consumers. That society had not the blank impersonality surrounding many of today's industries and services – whether in the hands of private or public, national or multinational companies, with their remote boards of directors – and was still quite close to the almost feudal attitudes of early Victorian entrepreneurs who took a paternal interest in the well-being of their employees but bore an implacable hostility, backed up by punitive measures, to any attempt by those employees to assert their independence as free men and women selling their working capacity in the labour market. Indeed, if anyone believes that trying to undermine the influence of the unions is peculiar to our times they have something to learn from the experience of the gasworkers of 1889, for, however enthusiastically welcomed by thousands upon thousands of general, low-paid workers, this new unionism was far from being greeted with universal acclaim.

Hyndman and the SDF

The most disconcerting opposition came from the leader of the Social-Democratic Federation: H.M. Hyndman. A difficult man despite his considerable political insight, he had a blind spot where trade unions were concerned, viewing with scepticism their value to the interests of the working class. It is true that in his early work, *England for All*, Hyndman in 1881 had paid lip service to reducing the hours of work, while his Social-Democratic Federation in 1884 had advocated the eight-hour day for government servants and, later, supported the principle of an Eight Hour Act; but it proposed – and engaged in – no activity or even propaganda to further that aim, Hyndman personally voicing his scornful opinion of trade unionists and all their works.

When Tom Mann protested against this cavalier attitude, urging that it was precisely socialists who should be able to appreciate the part trade unions could play, Hyndman rebuked him sharply, saying that the unions were led by:

> the most stodgy-brained, dull-witted, and slow-going time-servers in the country [and] to place reliance upon them, or to go out of our way to conciliate them, would be entirely wrong ...

This was in 1885 and Hyndman was, of course, referring to the leaders of the old craft unions. Nevertheless, when the New Unionism came into being, he entirely underestimated its significance, retaining his prejudice against the unions as such for all the days of his life. In 1911, writing his reminiscences, he said:

> Trade unions, by admitting wages as the permanent basis of the industrial system, virtually condemn their members to continuous toil for the benefit of the profit-takers ...

And he expressed himself even more forcibly in a letter to a friend:

> ... in fact, the trade unions ... stand in the way of a genuine organisation of the proletariat ...

It is small wonder that William Morris spoke of:

> all [Hyndman's] insane talk of immediate forcible revolution, when he knows that the workers of England are not even touched by the movement, hence ... the neglect of organisation ...

What Morris – and Eleanor Marx, and Will Thorne and Tom Mann and others behind the new trade unions – saw only too clearly was that no amount of preaching socialism would or could touch the ordinary working man and woman so long as they were condemned to toiling for twelve hours a day, without respite and without hope, until their brutalised and shortened lives came to an end. Thorne put it well when he wrote of the 'vague, indefinite appeals to revolution' made by propagandists. 'We,' he said, 'offered them' – the 'underpaid and oppressed workers' –

> something tangible, a definite, clearly-sighted road out
> of their misery ... It was this spirit of the New
> Unionism that made international working-class
> solidarity a reality ...

Significantly, in August 1889, hot upon the
victory of the gasworkers and just when the
Dock Strike was about to erupt, the Annual
Conference of the Social-Democratic Federation
revised its programme which made not a single
reference to trade unionism. While its new
rules appointed six committees to deal with the
various spheres of the Federation's activities,
industry was omitted altogether. Thus the most
progressive movement of the day, one to which
the young trade union should have been able to
look for support in word and deed was, if
anything, antagonistic and to all intents and
purposes silent, useless and inert.

The Trade Union Establishment

Less unexpected but nonetheless disheartening
was the attitude of the older established unions
to the newcomers who, in rejecting the
functions of a benefit society, seemed to be
passing judgment upon their methods.

This hostility to the new unions was to
manifest itself in many forms but most notably
in an article in the June 1890 issue of *Murray's
Magazine* by George Shipton, a former General

Secretary of the Society of London Amalgamated House Decorators and Painters – a member of 'the Junta' – and, for the past nineteen years, the Secretary of the London Trades Council. His article on trade unionism, old and new, was little more than a wide-ranging attack upon the new. He charged it with violating the voluntary principle in trying to assert the right to what was in effect the closed shop: a refusal to work with non-unionists; with fomenting rather than avoiding strikes; with striving to wring from the employers more money for less work – this last indictment coming strangely from any type of trade unionist, however hidebound – and, as though the new organisations were unique in this, Shipton pilloried them for not having won every action in which they had engaged during the short period of their existence. He further accused them of being led by 'outsiders' of the middle class, which was not only untrue but, in so far as people who could be so described had come to the aid and defence of the struggling new organisations, they had shamed the old school of working-class leaders who had failed to do so.

Immediately Tillett and Mann wrote a pamphlet in reply to Shipton, not fearing to attack his own somewhat dubious credentials:

East End labourers are not in George Shipton's line.

Constructing a retort house circa 1890

Picnics to the Channel Tunnel, Sandringham, and deputations in connection with various semi-politic and patriotic and demi-semi-trade unionist and pseudo-philanthropic movements ... are much more agreeable ...

He had been guilty, they pointed out, of blank indifference to the Dock Strike and, in an interview published in a London evening paper, had sneered at the new unions as 'mushroom' growths, doomed to an early demise: a prediction the more likely of fulfilment since, when asked to help general workers organise, he and his colleagues had refused on the grounds that such workers were not capable of organisation.

Tillett and Mann wrote:

Our trade unions shall be the centres of enlightenment, and not merely the meeting-place for paying contributions and receiving donations. The organisation of those who are classed as unskilled is of the most vital importance and must receive adequate attention; no longer can the skilled assume with a sort of superior air that they are the salt of the earth. The man or the woman who honestly toils, no matter in what capacity, is of the most vital concern to the community ... such is our belief and such is our policy ... and those who don't like it had better prepare at once their best weapons to meet us ...

Those weapons were wielded to some purpose three months later at the 1890 TUC, when the old guard defended its entrenched positions and defied the upstarts, whose contributions – even John Burns's trumpet voice (and he, after all, was a delegate not from the new unions, but from the old Amalgamated Society of Engineers) – were shouted down. But, as with all young things, time was on their side.

The Employers

Last, but of course the most powerful of opponents, there were the employers to whom, in those far-off, barbaric times, union-bashing came as second nature. Indeed, if one wishes to know exactly what Victorian values are so highly recommended in our own day, one has only to glance at the testimony given before the Royal Commission on Labour which began its work on 1 May 1891 'to enquire into the relations between employers and employed'.

Here will be found a witness who, having made enquiries among 'corporations and corporate bodies', elicited the general view that Acts of Parliament 'which allowed workers to combine' should be rescinded, making it 'impossible for them to use their influence'. This almost 70 years after the repeal of the Combination Acts. Another witness giving evidence – George Trewby, the chief engineer at Beckton – voiced, though less sweepingly, his disapproval of the Gasworkers' Union because, he complained, it called itself a 'fighting body'. 'It does not appear to have been like the old unions,' he lamented. 'We had no trouble whatever with them.'

While a Hyndman and a Shipton might express critical, even derogatory, views of the union, possibly harming it in the eyes of other workers and potential recruits, the employers alone had the capacity to break and destroy it. Only they fully understood the threat it represented to the system of overworking and underpaying unorganised labourers without hindrance in the interests of profit-making; and they reacted in accordance.

A generation earlier – in the late 1850s – there had been as many as thirteen gas companies in the metropolis. Now, in 1889, as a result of a series of mergers and what we should call take-overs, completed by 1883, there were, apart from the small Commercial company (established in 1833), only two: the Gas, Light & Coke Company – now under the Governorship of Colonel Sir William Makins, Conservative MP for Walthamstow – with ten works in central, east, west and north London; and the South Metropolitan Gas Company with six works south of the river in the Old Kent Road, Vauxhall, Rotherithe, Bankside and two in Greenwich.

The Chairman of the South Metropolitan

Company, which had been started in 1842, was in 1889 and had been for the past four years, George Livesey, born in 1834 and more or less brought up within the precincts of the gasworks, for his father had been the company's secretary since 1839. The son started work there at the age of fourteen, earning £50 a year. Now, at the age of 55, he had manoeuvred himself into absolute control of his board of directors and would tolerate no interference with nor challenge to his authority, least of all from his workers. A devious and cantankerous man of the highest moral and religious principles, he was on exceedingly bad terms with his opposite number, the Governor of the Gas, Light & Coke Company, upon whom he frequently made savage and quite unjustifiable personal attacks. Occasionally, however, he found it expedient to join forces when it came to the overriding common interest of putting down insubordinate subordinates.

Had these two powerful men not been at loggerheads at the moment when the union came into being it might well have been strangled at birth. As it was, the Gas, Light & Coke Company, after considering the matter, had recognised the justice of the demand and accorded the men the eight-hour shift system at the end of May, granting them, a month later, payment of time-and-a-half for Sunday work between 6 a.m. and 6 p.m.

Makins got a little of his own back by declining Livesey's proposal to meet and discuss the issue with a view to presenting a united front. The South Metropolitan was therefore obliged to act alone and according to its own lights, which it did to such good purpose that it provoked a costly strike before the year 1889 was out.

However, it had no alternative but to introduce the eight-hour day and extra payment for Sunday work. This it did, with bad grace and after some delay, in the second week of July, by which time almost all the stokers were organised. Early in September the union sought to enforce what was then its Rule 16 stating that 'all new hands ... to become Members of the Society before being permitted to start work', and posted up a notice proclaiming what was in effect a closed shop. The company riposted with its own notice announcing that it did not recognise the union, preferred non-union men and would protect them against any kind of threatening behaviour. Suiting its action to those words it sacked a Vauxhall stoker for attempting to recruit others to the union, accusing him of intimidation. His workmates demanded his immediate reinstatement and, although this was grudgingly promised, the men had no faith in that promise and proceeded to hand in their notices, whereupon the company caved in and took the man back. This was the first move in an undeclared war, as it were: an alarm signal, not lost upon Livesey.

In October Thorne began negotiations for double time to be paid for Sunday work not only until 6 p.m. but up to 10 p.m. starting in November. Livesey indignantly objected that this was a departure from the agreement reached only three months earlier and, while he refused point-blank to consider paying double time in any circumstances whatsoever, he allowed, under protest, that time-and-a-half should be extended to the additional four hours on Sunday evenings between six and ten, with the warning that he would reverse this agreement as soon as possible.

PIPE-CLEANER.

Outraged at having been forced to make one concession after another, Livesey, once he had recovered from the shock, began mustering his forces for the counter-attack. As early as the third week in September, as he later admitted, 'Preparations were actively and quietly made to meet the contingency of a strike.' He began to hold regular meetings with the managers of the various works to co-ordinate those preparations. Advertisements for labour were drafted with the instruction that they were to be inserted in London and provincial papers the moment the order was given by telegram. The company's agents were sent to scour the countryside to make enquiries about available men, while coal stocks were steadily built up. Quantities of beds and bedding, as well as steam cauldrons for heating food, were ordered for delivery at short notice and corrugated iron hutments, to serve as temporary accommodation, were made ready.

Livesey personally called upon the Commissioner of Police – who shared his view that a failure in the supply of gas would be an even greater disaster than the damage done to the capital by the dockers' strike – and he agreed that the maximum police help and protection should be given in the event of a gasworkers' strike. In after years Livesey wrote:

One Wednesday in October 1889 ... the chief foreman ... said to me: 'The stokers are all in the Union and we have lost all authority in the retort houses ... Unless you do something to attach them to the Company we shall be completely in the power of the Union.' In a

quarter of an hour the scheme was set out ... and the
same afternoon it was offered to the workmen. The
Union men refused it ... and on November 4th
demanded that ... it be abolished ... Then the
memorable strike began: thus was our Co-partnership
born ...

That may not be a strictly accurate account of
the matter but it is true that Livesey launched
his bonus scheme – under the misnomers
'Co-partnership' and 'Profit-sharing' – on a day
that fell between two dates when the employers
were to meet the union to negotiate a
settlement of the Sunday
pay question.

The terms on offer were
1 per cent of a year's
wages to be paid for every
penny that the price of
gas fell below 2s 8d per
thousand cubic feet. This
was not quite as simple as
it sounds. It had the flaw
of being a pure gamble
since the cost of gas-
making was inevitably
tied to the price of its raw
material – coal – over
which, even if it owned a
single colliery here or
there, no gas company

SCOOP·DRIVER.

— 110 —

could exercise control. A further inducement was that the bonus was to be back-dated three years, yielding a so-called 'nest-egg' of 8 per cent. In the year 1889, this would represent some £7 for each worker, not to be touched, however, for five years. In return the men were to sign a contract binding themselves to remain in the company's service for twelve months during which time they undertook not to go on strike or to cause 'any wilful injury' to the firm, to remain 'sober, honest and industrious', to obey the foremen in every particular and in no circumstances to leave without the express consent of the engineer. The scheme was openly recognised by both sides as a move to encourage the men to leave the union in exchange for a bribe to accept feudal conditions of tied labour.

Many of the yardmen, most of whom were unorganised, signed the agreement within a fortnight. The stokers on the other hand met Livesey to demand the withdrawal of the whole scheme. Thorne, after consulting his Executive, attempted to bargain on the details: the bonus should be included in the weekly pay-packet, the percentage should be higher and the waiting-time shorter for the 'nest-egg' to be paid out, while the compulsory twelve months' contract and the no-strike clauses were completely unacceptable. At a mass meeting held during the third week of November, the entire scheme was condemned, as Thorne went back to tell Livesey. Certain modifications were then introduced by the company and the revised version of the deal was posted up in the works. The no-strike condition was withdrawn, the 'nest-egg' earning was increased from 8 to 9 per cent and the waiting time to draw it reduced from five to three years. The men would still be 'bound hand and foot', as Thorne put it, and this remained a prohibitive condition in his view.

However, at that stage three men in the carbonising department of the Vauxhall works signed the amended agreement and tore up their union cards. Thorne wrote to Livesey demanding that those men be removed from the retort house. If they were not, all the stokers would walk out. Livesey refused. 'We had been watching our opportunity,' he openly admitted at a later date, 'and we saw it on receipt of this letter.'

A day later, on 5 December 1889, some 2,000 South Metropolitan workers – almost all the stokers and many of the yardmen – handed in their notices. This gave Livesey the vital time needed to put his well-laid plans into operation. The strike which he had not merely foreseen but to all intents and purposes had engineered, was on.

All this and much more was disclosed at the hearings of the Royal Commission on Labour when Livesey – who served on its panel and was allowed great latitude in questioning the trade union witnesses, including Thorne – was himself examined by Anthony Mundella, the President of the Board of Trade, a progressive Liberal and staunch supporter of trade unionism, who was responsible for introducing the first Courts of Conciliation to settle disputes between masters and men. Livesey made no bones about his aims: he wished to prevent men from joining the union and induce them to leave it if they had become members. He further revealed that, when he had largely failed in this – though not without successfully splitting the union's ranks – he had resorted to the most draconian methods.

It was a bitter strike in bitter weather, lasting some eight weeks. With the aid of the railway companies, non-union men were brought to London from half-a-dozen counties, to be taken under massive police escort to the makeshift housing prepared for their reception. On the first day no fewer than 600 police, including 80 mounted, were on guard to protect the scabs in the Vauxhall works from the fury of the strikers, whose pickets were not only unable to approach or speak to them but had to be withdrawn in face of the violence of the police who clearly had their instructions and laid about them with a will. They ended by arresting no fewer than 40 men who were found guilty of assault.

For their further protection the strike-breakers were given full board on the company's premises. It is interesting that Livesey, a devout teetotaller who would not allow strong drink in his works, made an exception for scabs: unlimited beer flowed in the shanties where they were lodged and which nightly resounded to the clamour of wild drunkenness. This did not improve their performance in the retort house on the next morning.

The truth is that stokers, those unskilled workers as they were denigratingly called, needed to be not only extremely muscular and hardy but to have acquired a high degree of technical proficiency, not to mention dexterity, if they were to avoid accidents and injury. Such skill, whatever it may have been called, was not to be picked up in a day or two. Obviously the newcomers, unemployed men from the streets and the countryside, unused to the gruelling physical conditions and the punishing exertions of stoking, were pretty useless at the start. Working together with trained men they could have learnt quite quickly; as it was, it took them at least a fortnight, during which many of them suffered severe burns, to master the job. Indeed, although Livesey re-imposed the twelve-hour shift system as soon as the strike broke out, it was not until well into January that production reached anything approaching the required level.

In the meantime the effects began to tell on south London households, which were advised to economise their use of gas. Many went back to using oil lamps while street lighting in some areas was reduced by an hour both night and early morning, despite the dark and foggy winter.

On strike pay of 10 shillings a week for as long as the union could afford it and then reduced to 5 shillings (though one paper reported that the union had raised this to 12s 6d early in January, not elsewhere confirmed), instead of the regular earnings of an average £1 15s, the men and their families experienced great hardship. Stokers were not, in fact, among the lowest paid, since the labourer of that time earned roughly £1 5s. Stokers were thus fully acknowledged as, at the very least, semi-skilled.

The sad fact was that, unlike that of the dockers,

A DOOR-MAN.

— 115 —

this strike attracted little sympathy. Indeed, with the return to a normal gas supply, the general public and the press, from having been hostile, lost all interest: a circumstance that heralded the beginning of the end and the defeat of the union. Worse than the general indifference was the lack of support from other unions. Only the Coal Porters' and the Seamen's & Firemen's unions came out and, though at mass meetings there was brave talk of 'concerted action', nothing came of it. Most mortifyingly, the dockers, whom the gasworkers had backed to the hilt with speakers and money and clerical assistance, gave no help at all. That the craft unions should not make common cause with the labourers came as no surprise, but the lack of solidarity was none the less fatal.

Thorne appealed to the London Trades Council for support, but was advised by George Shipton – who would later attack the union publicly for its failure to win this strike – to seek a settlement on the best terms he could get. There was plainly no alternative. Thus, on 25 January Thorne asked Shipton to open negotiations with the South Metropolitan. Agreement was reached and a settlement signed on 4 February. On the following day the strike was called off, the company undertaking to revert to the eight-hour shift system and to give all former employees the opportunity to be re-engaged without fear of victimisation.

On that second condition Livesey simply went back upon his word. Addressing a Plymouth audience ten days after the end of the strike Thorne was reported in a local paper to have said that London gas users should be warned that the men would never again give seven days' notice of a strike, nor yet a day. This was kindly brought to Livesey's attention and he seized upon it to display notices outside the works announcing: 'No Union Men Need Apply'.

In point of fact, at a South Metropolitan Directors' Meeting held only four days after the strike started, it was stated: 'It has been the rule of the company for at least fifty years that men who strike leave the company without hope of return.' (This recalls Bernard Shaw's observation in a different context that 'The passage of time does not consecrate a tradition, it makes an anachronism of it.') It was thus plain that Livesey had had no need for the slender pretext of Thorne's speech and, moreover, it also emerged that in the brief period between the signing of the settlement and the report of Thorne's words appearing in the *Western Morning News* – a matter of less than a fortnight – Livesey had broken the terms of the agreement by taking on outsiders and refusing jobs to the union men who had worked there previously. Nor was this enough for him: he blacklisted them, making it difficult for them to get work elsewhere.

The suffering cannot be assessed. In cash terms, the strike cost the union something in the order of £1,250 a week and continued to be paid for five weeks after the strike was officially at an end. The whole amount was subsequently – and variously – said to have been £9,000, £10,000 or £12,000. It cost the company either £100,000, as Livesey claimed or, according to Thorne, £250,000. Either way, Livesey considered it well worth the money since it had driven the union out of his works. He was also rewarded by the enthusiastic congratulations and a handsome cheque from the shareholders in the company. This money, after making a donation to police funds, he naturally devoted to the benefit of the poor.

Presenting his Second Half-yearly Report and Balance Sheet in April 1890 Thorne said:

> We have been told that our union is crippled, we admit that the strike dealt us a severe blow, but we have consolation in the fact that we fought well ...

And, opening the First Annual Conference on 19 May, he declared:

> Mr Livesey has spoken of 'smashing' the union. This

Conference is the best answer to him. Everywhere, in every part of the Kingdom the Masters are trying to crush this union. Where other Unions are tolerated, ours is attacked. Those among us who are known to be members of the Union … are being weeded out. Unless we look out, the eight hours we have won will be taken from us. So we must stand firm and fight for our Union and the cause of the workers … We have a great fight to fight. Let us fight it together …

Though battered by the experience of this and other strikes which erupted in the provinces – not always with official union sanction – the gasworkers' organisation not only survived but thrived to see this day, one hundred years later.

III

Forerunners

Although this union was the only one to live and flourish it was by no means the first that gasworkers had tried to organise. Indeed, there had been no fewer than nine earlier attempts: small, weak and short-lived, it is true, but for all that a true badge of courage for those involved. Here is a brief history of their efforts. It is a moving story of a struggle waged against tremendous odds under conditions different at each stage from those prevailing in 1889, but nevertheless akin in reflecting the will of an oppressed and browbeaten body of men to assert their independence of spirit.

It must be recalled that, following the repeal of the Combination Acts in 1824, while trade unions were no longer illegal, practically anything they did rendered their members liable to prosecution. This remained so for another half century, despite the Trade Union Act of 1871. Thus, though a strike was lawful,

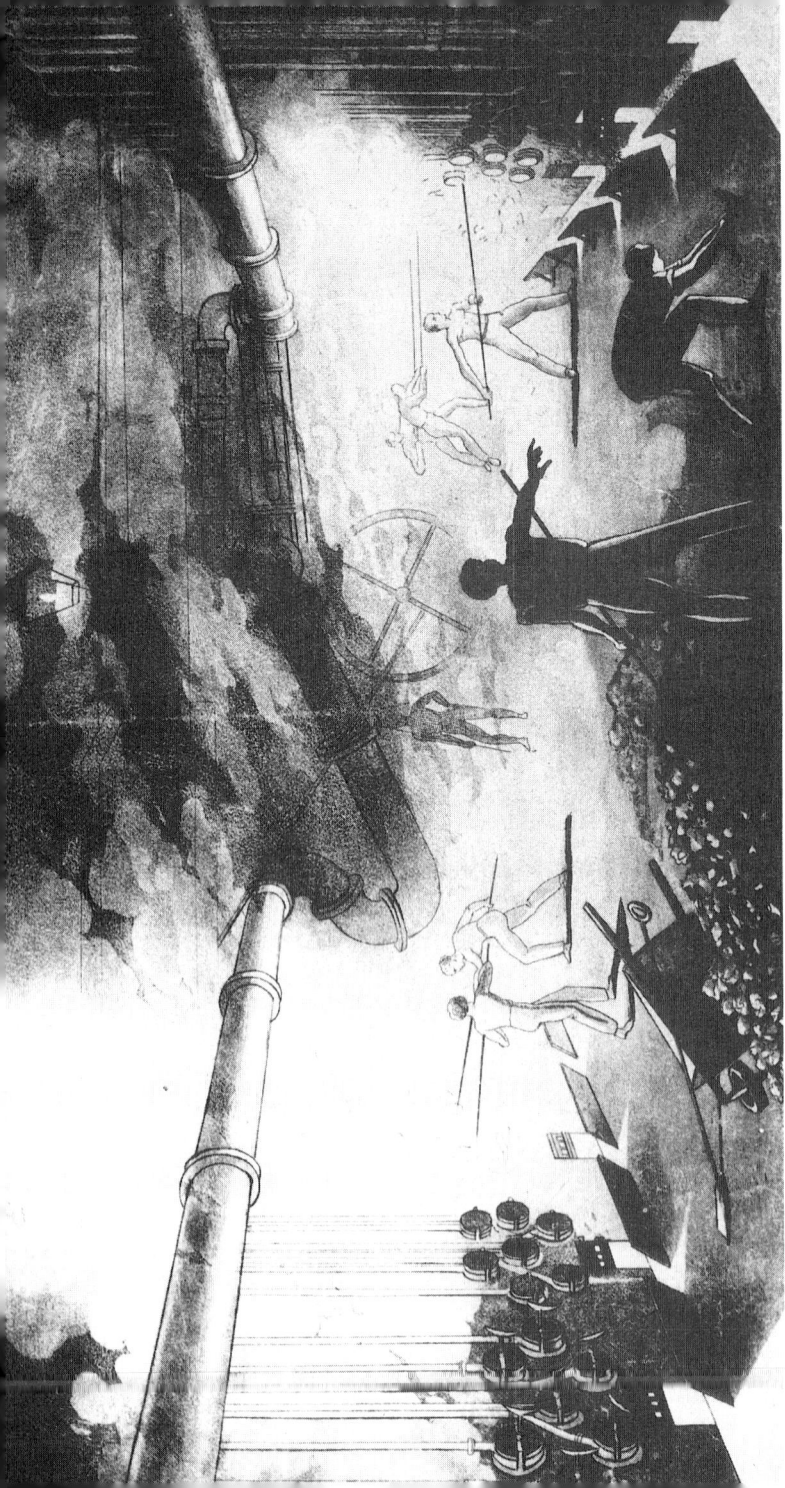

Brick Lane Works. Chartered Gas Co. 1821

steps taken to promote it constituted a criminal offence; workers who so much as prepared for a combined withdrawal of labour were deemed guilty of conspiracy which carried the penalty of a year's imprisonment. Again, an employer could break his contract by summarily dismissing a man or woman without facing anything worse than a possible – though rather unlikely – suit for damages when, in any case, he was able to give evidence in his defence; but a worker who left his job without notice could be sentenced to three months in jail and was not allowed to bear witness on his own behalf. Justices of the Peace could issue warrants for the arrest of a worker on the uncorroborated word, if given on oath, by his employer; he could be plucked from his bed and sent to prison by a magistrate who, as like as not, was himself a local employer of labour. They were without question bold men who defied laws so heavily weighted against them.

The earliest recorded instance of united action by gasworkers took place in 1825, a year of booming trade in Britain, when the gas industry was relatively young. The stokers and labourers employed by the Chartered company – the name by which in its early years the Gas, Light & Coke company was known – and the Imperial company struck for a pay rise. Despite the legislation so recently enacted the men were not, in fact, organised and could therefore be picked off one by one. All those who went on strike were sacked and, by way of warning, twelve of them were arrested, though charges were later dropped.

Both companies had recruited strike-breakers not only among rural populations but also in the town's workhouses. They also circulated the names of strikers to other employers to prevent them getting work elsewhere and at the same time to the Poor Law guardians so that those men would be refused outdoor relief, thus deliberately and ruthlessly condemning them and their families to starvation. This set the pattern for subsequent disputes. In most instances the effect of such vengeful action long outlasted its cause since the workers' various actions were speedily defeated as a rule.

In February 1834 (barely a month, as it happened, before the six famous agricultural labourers of Tolpuddle were tried for 'administering unlawful oaths' – that is, trying to form a trade union – and were sentenced to seven years transportation) some 150 gasworkers in the Chartered company started a union and tried to make theirs a closed shop. The next month 35 of them went to the employers asking for a wage increase of 7 shillings a week. At that time stokers earned £1 8s and labourers

£1 1s. The company's response was to rid themselves of the men who had voiced the demand and replace them with non-unionists. A few days later 80 of the men in another of the company's works made the same wage claim, were refused, walked out and were dismissed. The movement spread from one gasworks to another whose several directors thereupon got together to co-ordinate their tactics, which were of the simplest and most direct: they sacked all identifiable trade unionists, blacklisted them, imported non-union labour and appealed to the Home Secretary for police protection.

Having taken on untrained – genuinely unskilled – workers, the gas companies were obliged to advise their customers that there might be a failure in the gas supply and, indeed, on 8 March 1834, a Saturday, the Strand was plunged into darkness.

The outcome of this first valiant but fruitless effort to organise was that over 2,000 stokers were thrown out of work. The union lasted no more than a fortnight. There was not another attempt for 25 years.

In February 1859 the Loyal Gas Stokers' Protective Society was formed with the aim of winning a reduction of working hours from twelve to ten and an increase of 1 shilling a day, to bring the wage up to £1 15s a week. The 50 or so men on the day shift at the Horseferry Road

The Air of Freedom

Horseferry Road, 11th March, 1834.

The Chartered Gas Company beg leave to acquaint their Customers and the Public, that they have been compelled to discharge their Workmen, because they threatened to strike unless one of their brethren of the Union was again taken into employ who had been discharged for drunkenness, and for subsequently using the same threat, unless Five Men, (not Unionists) were discharged, who had been recently taken into the Company's service.

They wish also to add, that although so sudden a change of Workmen necessarily embarrassed them for a moment, the new hands are becoming used to the work, and an ample supply of Gas may now be expected.

C. F. SEYFANG, Printer, 57 Farringdon Street,

Leaflet distributed by the Chartered Gas Company to its customers

Westminster works of the Chartered company placed their claim before the employer who turned them down. The men then walked out and strikes spread throughout the industry, lasting some four months.

On that occasion the company had been taken by surprise and was unprepared, so that it found itself obliged to make some concession on wages, but it swiftly recovered the high ground, fell back upon the expedients of blacklisting and refusing to re-employ anyone who had struck and then confronted the workers with a document which read:

THE Consumers of Gas are earnestly requested by the Gas Companies to burn the Gas as moderately as possible for a few Nights, and especially this Evening *(Saturday)* in consequence of a Combination among the Men employed in the various Gas Works.

Gas Works, Horseferry Road,
March 8, 1834.

W. GLINDON, Printer, 51, Rupert Street, Haymarket.

Leaflet distributed by the Chartered Gas Company to its customers

> I am not and will not while in the service of the company be a member of, or in any way belong to, any trade union or association having for its object the reduction of hours of labour or the restriction or limitation of work.

Since the alternative to signing this undertaking was unemployment, more than half the men signed. The few who refused to do so were dismissed. By July the Society with its high-sounding title and moderate objectives had disappeared without trace. It had lasted a bare six months.

As before, when strike-breakers were

brought in, the companies enlisted the help of the police and local magistrates to protect the scabs, who were fed and housed on company premises for their own safety. It will be seen that whatever virtues George Livesey of the South Metropolitan Gas Company displayed in the strike of 1889, originality was not one of them.

A Stokers' Association came briefly into existence in August 1867. It set out, like its predecessor, to reduce the hours of work: this time to eight, a demand so popular that 1,000 men – reckoned to be a quarter of all London stokers at the time – attended the Assocation's first public meeting. A petition was drawn up and presented to the companies who rejected it out of hand. The men thereupon revised the claim, asking for a half-day off on Saturdays and the payment of time-and-a-half for Sunday work. They were granted a slight reduction of hours for Sundays, but their other demands were not met. The organisation faded away. However, on the basis of the small concession won, a vigorous movement sprang up a few years later for the total abolition of Sunday work without a reduction of pay or, alternatively, double-time rates for all Sunday hours.

Some of the older men who were to support Thorne in 1889 may well have known or heard

The Loyal Gas Stokers Protective Society was formed at the Westminster Works in 1859; this print of the retort house was published in 1860.

tell of the London & Metropolitan Gas Stokers', Fitters', Smiths', and Yardmen's Amalgamated Society, launched in August 1872 to press for this amelioration of conditions. The Chartered company, now known as the Gas, Light & Coke, responded to the union's claim by calling a meeting of the other London companies. It was agreed that certain wage increases should be granted and the Society went ahead with its case for the abolition of Sunday work (or double-time payment) with both the Chartered and the Imperial companies. The former decided to concede a further small wage increase; the latter simply ignored the whole thing.

Early in October 150 men on the Sunday night shift walked out. This was, however, without the Society's backing, and they were shortly persuaded to return to work. At the end of that month, the union was strongly represented at a public meeting where the case for the total abolition of Sunday work was put with great force, speaker after speaker condemning the practice of carbonisers working twelve-hour shifts, week in, week out, throughout the entire year.

Trouble began a month later when, convinced of the justice of their case, the Society was determined to assert itself and the employers were equally resolute to break it. In this struggle, though some of the men paid a heavy price, the union and its allies succeeded in winning vital changes in the laws governing their status.

On Friday, 30 November, a trade unionist who worked in the coking section of the Imperial company's Fulham works was arbitrarily sacked and replaced by a non-union man. The organised stokers in the carbonising department took up the question of his reinstatement, whereupon the management locked out two of the stoking gangs that same night.

Events then moved swiftly. At the Beckton works of the Chartered company a trade unionist named Dilley was ordered by the foreman to instruct and work with a couple of untrained and, in his view, incompetent, non-union navvies. He refused and was sacked. On the following day, a Sunday, 1 December, a general meeting of the Society was held on Clerkenwell Green at which it was resolved that the Secretary, Webster, should meet the Fulham management to pursue the matter of reinstating the locked-out stokers and, if this failed, the members would demonstrate their solidarity with those men. Twice Webster and a deputation attempted to see the management, without success.

The next day stokers in all the London

gasworks – some 2,500 – came out on strike. In a few retort houses the entire workforce stayed away. At a delegate meeting held in a Finsbury pub on the day after, it was reported that, though the men would have preferred to adhere to the union's rules by giving due notice before walking out, they had been forced to contravene them owing to the companies' provocation. Their secretary and the deputation that had sought an interview had, in addition, been grossly insulted. It was also reported that one of the managers at the Imperial company's Hackney works had asserted that the companies would crush the union even if it cost them a million pounds.

On Wednesday, 4 December, a meeting took place in Trafalgar Square attended by about 4,000 gas workers. The numerous instances of victimisation were described by the speakers and a resolution was passed calling for the full reinstatement of the Fulham workers. It was proposed that the question of Sunday working should be submitted to arbitration.

The Chartered company called its directors together on the next day when it was unanimously agreed that arbitration should be refused and that no men who had struck should be taken back. In their invincible hostility to the union they were prepared to go to any lengths and they now instructed their managers to take out and hold in reserve summonses against the strikers, while scabs were brought to London from as far afield as Plymouth.

A week had now passed and, by 7 December, the companies were advising consumers to reduce their use of gas in the period when the new workers were learning the job. By the end of another week, it looked as though the men's position was hopeless: they had not only failed to win public sympathy, owing to the inconvenience of a reduction in the domestic gas supply, but they were being relentlessly hunted down: many strikers were brought to court and sentenced to hard labour. At that point – 10 December – six stokers were charged with

> unlawfully, wickedly and maliciously conspiring together ... to reinstate another workman named Dilley in his employment after he had been lawfully and for sufficient reason discharged; secondly, for committing breaches of their contract; and thirdly, for intimidating others to do likewise.

The six were sent for trial.

One man disappeared and could not be traced; the other five, including Dilley himself – John Barnes, George Ray, Robert Wilson and Edmond Jones – came up before Mr Justice Brett (later the first Lord Esher) and a jury at the Old Bailey on 18 December. They were found guilty of breaking the Criminal Law Amendment Act of 1871 and the Master and

GREAT GRIMSBY GAS WORKS

RULES AND REGULATIONS.

1st.—All Stokers, Labourers, and other Workmen employed on these Works must at all times, day or night, enter and leave the Works by way of Sheepfold-street only.

2nd.—No Workman or Workmen, except Stokers and Lamplighters, will be allowed to leave the Works on any pretence whatsoever between the hours of 6 and 8 a.m.; 8-30 a.m. and 12 noon; or 1 and 5-30 p.m. without the knowledge, leave, or consent of the Manager or Foreman.

3rd.—No Workman or other person will be allowed to take Coke out of the Works without having it weighed and properly entered, and no Coke or any article whatsoever is to be taken from the Works between the hours of 5-30 p.m. and 6 a.m.; neither will any Workman be allowed to take Coke out during work hours, but he may have it loaded and weighed ready for the time he leaves work.

4th.—The times for Meals shall be as follow, viz.:—Breakfast, 8 to 8-30 a.m.; Dinner, 12 to 1 noon; except under special circumstances.

5th.—Smoking strictly prohibited in all buildings and other parts of the Works but the Retort-house, and there allowed to Stokers only, except at meal times.

6th.—Any Workman or Workmen known to infringe or found infringing any of the foregoing Rules and Regulations will render himself liable to immediate dismissal.

NOTE.—Stokers' time defined in their special Rules, and Lamplighters will follow the usual course.

These harsh conditions were laid down for men still on the twelve-hour day. Undated works notice.

Servant Act of 1867, for which the maximum penalty was three months' imprisonment. Nevertheless, though the jury recommended the men to mercy as poor, ignorant fellows who had been led astray, they were convicted and sentenced to a year's hard labour.

There was a public outcry at the severity of the punishment. A defence committee was set up and met every Saturday afternoon at the offices of the *Bee-Hive*, the weekly journal of the trade union movement. It sent a Memorial to the Home Secretary on 7 January appealing for a remission of the sentences. This had no immediate effect; but when Mr Justice Brett was consulted by the authorities he, while defending his verdict, took the view that if the men themselves were to express contrition, they might be granted clemency. This opinion was conveyed to their solicitor who advised them to sign a joint petition couched in penitent terms. They did so. They had been suffering above all other tribulations from the intense cold of their prison cells after having been so long accustomed to the overheated atmosphere of the retort houses.

On 31 January 1873 the Home Secretary, Henry Bruce, remitted the sentences to four months and the men were released from Maidstone County Gaol on 15 April to tremendous acclaim by a great demonstration.

Arising from this case and the widespread indignation it had aroused a vigorous agitation for changes in the law was mounted, leading eventually, in 1875, to the unconditional repeal of the former harshly discriminatory measures and the passing of the Conspiracy and Protection of Property Act and the Employers and Workmen Act, which abolished imprisonment for breach of contract, permitted peaceful picketing and treated employers and workers as equal partners to a civil contract. By the terms of the new Acts, workers in gas and water undertakings were forbidden to strike.

Interestingly enough, Mr Justice Brett, whose 'vindictive sentence' on the gasworkers, as the Webbs called it, had been denounced by one of the union leaders as 'atrocious' and reminiscent of the 'evil days of Judge Jeffreys', welcomed the new legislation.

Not so the employers. Fearing the effects it could have in curbing their authority when it reached the statute book, they founded the National Federation of Associated Employers of Labour in 1873 which held its first meeting on 24 February 1875. It recognised that more sophisticated methods of exercising control over the workforce and combatting trade union influence would have to be adopted.

So far as the London & Metropolitan Amalgamated Society was concerned, although the most outstanding attempt yet made to organise in the gas industry, it failed, like every other, to stay the course. The membership trickled away and the old fear of victimisation and prosecution – despite the reduced opportunities for the one and the milder penalties now involved in the other – reasserted itself.

Undeterred however, yet another Workers' Amalgamated Society sprang up in 1881. This was formally entered with the Registrar of Friendly Societies, but it did not last. Three years later, another union – the Association of Gasworkers of the United Kingdom – was started, this time in secret, only to collapse after a few weeks. The next year a similar move was made, supported by relatively few men. It fizzled out in a matter of months.

At the turn of the year 1886-87 1,000 recruiting leaflets were distributed in London by a newly-formed organisation calling itself the Amalgamated Association of Gas Workers of the United Kingdom. This was based entirely on Beckton, where Thorne was working, and he became a Trustee of the Association. It gained little support from other than a handful of socialists and numbered fewer than 50 members. It lasted barely eight months, but it had been registered so that when, in June 1889, Thorne applied to the Registrar of Friendly Societies, he was not able to use the same title.

'A.S. of Gas Stokers of the United Kingdom meeting held at the Sir John Lawrence, Canning Town on May 13, 1887. Minutes. Proposed by Mr County, sec. by Mr Thorne that this society be still continued. Proposed by Mr Thorne sec. M. Smith that we meet fortnightly on the Friday night. Both carried.'
Minutes of the Amalgamated Society of Gas Stokers, 3 May, 1887.

Thus the name of the National Union of Gas Workers and General Labourers of Great Britain and Ireland came to be adopted.

One of the apparently insuperable obstacles to a stable organisation was, of course, the seasonal nature of gasworking, and also the vulnerability of the men – unlike craftsmen – to being replaced with relative ease. Many of the same workers might be taken on, year after year, for the winter months, but many were not. The workforce was, of necessity, a fluctuating population and those who drifted away when the retort houses closed down – to the brickfields or other, often casual work – did not even consider themselves the stuff of trade unionists. Who, indeed, at that time had ever heard of an established trade union that catered for workers of that stamp?

IV
When,
Where, Why and Who

It may well be asked how it came about that, with this long history of brave attempts doomed to failure and defeat, again and again, a genuine and lasting union was successfully founded by the gasworkers in 1889.

The Britain of that period – two years after Queen Victoria's Golden Jubilee – exhibited certain distinctive features, not the least significant of which was that it was in the midst of the Great Depression, lasting roughly from 1870 until the turn of the century. It was marked by troughs of severe unemployment, wage reductions and stagnation – if not decline – in trade unionism, alternating with brief upswings of economic recovery and rapid expansion, notably that which occurred in the years 1887 to 1892, when some industrialists went so far as to complain that labour was scarce.

Britain's position in the world had vastly changed since the days when the brilliant scientific and industrial inventions of her gifted sons had made her supreme among nations; gone, too, were the twenty odd years when she exercised that supremacy unchallenged as the workshop of the world which had transformed the face of her towns and cities, drawing her people away from the fields and out of the villages. She was now, since 1870, confronted by the fierce competition of her European neighbours, not only in manufacteries but in the even more bitter rivalry to obtain an exclusive hold upon those distant parts of the earth that yielded raw materials, cheap labour and fresh markets.

In the decade 1881 to 1891, during which the number of agricultural workers fell by nearly 90,000, urban populations throughout the country went on growing; though in London, with its 4,500,000 inhabitants, there was a significant shift in location.

By the Local Government Act of 1888, the Metropolitan Board of Works was superseded by the London County Council which was to hold its very first meeting at precisely the same time – March 1889 – as the Gasworkers' Union came into being. The new administrative area, though it absorbed many parts of Middlesex, Surrey and Kent, did not include the outer ring of suburbs: places such as West Ham, Tottenham, Willesden and Leyton, where the population increased by some 50 per cent in those ten years. This was owed in part to the development of local industries, to increased travel facilities – the Cheap Trains Act of 1883 introduced workmen's tickets between 6 p.m. and 8 a.m. – but even more to the fact that dwellings and whole residential quarters in the old, central districts of the capital, and in particular the City, were now replaced by offices, banks and business premises of all kinds.

Modern Londoners will be amused to know that for those who still lived and worked in the metropolitan districts there were no fewer than twelve postal deliveries each day. Letters, posted in the area, if correctly addressed and bearing their penny stamp, reached their destination within two to four hours. In seven other less central areas, there were only between six and seven deliveries, while mail from London to the provinces was collected half-a-dozen times a day.

But then, this was a world without telephones, though they were well on the way. Unlike the outstanding discoveries of an earlier epoch, the telephone was not invented in Britain but in America. However, by 1878 a telephone company was established in London and in 1881, when a submarine cable was laid between a suburb of Calais and St Margarets in Kent as part of the line to connect London and Paris, its trials enabled Londoners to listen to the Paris opera, complete with the audience's applause and cries of '*bis!*' from which the English learnt to their surprise that the French do not shout '*encore!*'.

The other invention of the period coming on stream, as we should now put it, was electricity. Developments and improvements carried out in the decade 1870 to 1880 led to electric lighting being experimentally tried out in the West India Dock in 1877 and, a year later, at both the Gaiety Theatre and the Palace of Westminster. In 1879 it was proposed that streets, public buildings and factories should be entirely lit by electricity, for which pavements in London were taken up and 137 miles of cables were laid. In November that year the American, Thomas Edison, patented in Britain his incandescent electric light bulb; at which point the government had its attention drawn to the possibility of legislating on the subject and a Select Committee of the House of Commons was appointed, to consider whether it was:

> desirable to authorise municipal corporations or other local authorities to adopt any schemes for lighting by electricity.

A year later it reported that:

> ... energy of one horse-power may be converted into gaslight and yield a luminosity equal to 12-candle-power. But the same amount of energy transformed into electric light produces 1,600-candle-power ... Compared with gas, the economy for equal illumination does not yet appear to be conclusively established ... Gas companies ... have no special claim to be considered as the future distributors of electric light ...

Understandably all this had, one might say, an electrifying effect upon the gas companies, throwing them into a near panic and depressing the value of their shares on the stock market to an alarming extent. Ever since gas had superseded the age-old use of tallow and oil, the public had had no alternative form of lighting nor the companies any competition. The number of consumers had increased year by year, reaching over 300,000 in London after the introduction in 1887 of the domestic penny-in-the-slot meter and the Welsbach incandescent gas-mantle.

An Electrical Congress had been held in Paris in 1881 which laid down and adopted for all time such standard, international terms as ohm, ampère, watt and volt (after the German physicist George Simon Ohm, the French mathematician André Marie Ampère, the Scottish inventor James Watt and the Italian physicist Alessandro Volta), for measuring electrical resistance, pressure, units of power and current. The Electric Lighting Act of 1882, following the Select Committee's report, marked the end of what could be called the trial period – during which John Burns drove an electric tramcar round the grounds of the Crystal Palace for six months in 1881, by way of demonstration – and by 1888, when the Act was amended, the London Electricity Supply Corporation works at Deptford started to provide the entire metropolis with electric lighting. Indeed, early in 1889 the City, from Fleet Street to Aldgate, was so lit.

By this time electric trams were plying regularly in London and carrying some 56,000,000 passengers annually; while an electric train that ran beneath the Thames from the Monument to Clapham – having a dire effect, upon the instruments in Greenwich Observatory – was opened to the public at the end of 1890.

At this juncture the number of men in work in Great Britain (that is, England, Wales and Scotland) had risen to over 10,000,000 – the highest figure ever known – and to 4,500,000 women, out of a population of 31,000,000, while those employed in gas, water and sanitary undertaking had increased over the past twenty years (since 1871) from 25,000 to 60,000: a far higher rate of growth than that in

general employment. 45,000 people were working in the gas industry alone, inside and outside
the gas-making works, while by 1892 that had
risen to 70,000.

Those two decades saw the greatest expansion in the number of trade unions also: from 34
in 1871 they rose to 274 in 1891, the
membership increasing from 300,000 to well
over 1,500,000 of which the most notable
increase took place between 1889 and 1891.

The Royal Commission on Labour, to which
earlier references have been made, sat for two
years and was of considerable importance to the
industrial relations of the period. Despite the
presence on its panel of trade unionists –
including Tom Mann – it was heavily weighted
against wage-earners in that the employers
were supported at the hearings by lawyers,
economists and every kind of specialist consult-
ant whereas the trade unionists were not
allowed to call on expert advisers. Nevertheless, the Commission came to the conclusion
that industry as a whole had reached that stage
of development in which disputes were found to
be most frequent and most bitter where firms
were just, or not quite, emerging from what the
report called 'the patriarchal condition',
wherein the individual employer, oblivious to
the changing times still believed that he could
run his own establishment and govern his own

Double gang of stokers at Stepney Works at the turn of the century

workforce with no interference from unions or any other outside agency.

The Third Reform Act of 1884-85 had added some 2,000,000 voters at once to the franchise. In fact, they rose from approximately 3,000,000 in 1881, or 88 men in a thousand, to almost 6,800,000 in 1898, or 161 in a thousand, (demonstrating that many men and, of course, all women were still without the vote until 1918). The new voters included many miners, farmworkers and others of the working class, which fact exercised a certain influence upon the attitude of those employers who went in for enlightened self-interest. It explains the relative willingness of the more reasonable gas companies to accede to the powerful agitation of the newly-formed union for the eight-hour day, apart from the South Metropolitan which gave an exemplary display of the 'patriarchal condition'.

Another factor of even greater relevance to the success of the union, and a contributory element to the changing climate, was the revival of socialism. Hyndman's Democratic Federation, as it was originally called when he founded it in 1881, adopted a fully socialist programme in January 1884 and at its fourth Annual Conference in August that year it was renamed the Social-Democratic Federation. But before the year ended its most progressive members, including Eleanor Marx, under the leadership of William Morris, rebelled against Hyndman's arrogant, aggressive and contentious manner of ruling the organisation, which he tended to treat as his private property, and they left it to form the Socialist League.

Over the next five years various committed socialists hived off to start their own little splinter groups, sometimes with fewer members than would nowadays be thought to constitute a healthy local branch. It must be realised that, a hundred years ago, the total adherents to these assorted factions, including the Fabians who founded their society in 1884, did not amount to more than a handful. Their importance lay certainly not in their numbers but in their dedication and their influence. It was they who, with their vision of a better life, their fighting spirit and unquenchable hope, broke through the apathy and submissiveness of their more timid fellows.

It is easy to sneer at these tiny reservoirs of socialist men and women; easier still to decry their inability to show a united front to their capitalist opponents: the fact is that when, thanks to the efforts of a committee of which Will Thorne was the organising secretary, the first May Day, called to demand the eight-hour working day, was celebrated in 1890, the most gigantic demonstration ever witnessed assembled in Hyde Park: no fewer than 80 organisations jointly, even if not in combination, took part, representing trade unions of every shade of opinion, women's organisations, radical clubs, socialist societies, leagues and federations, Fabians, trades councils, LCC councillors and even progressive School Boards. From seven platforms the speakers from these diverse bodies addressed the mighty crowd of some 300,000.

Behind the reawakening of socialist aims and ideas and its spread among ordinary workers lay the direct experience of militant agitation and solidarity in support of the unemployed in the immediately preceding period, culminating in the battle of Trafalgar Square, known as Bloody Sunday, in 1887. It is not without interest that Canon Barnett – the founder in 1884 of Toynbee Hall – and his wife, both renowned for their philanthropy, could pontificate on the unemployed in terms, familiar enough today, with reference to that occasion:

> The very fact of industrial progress tends to throw out of work those unfitted by health, education or character to reach the high level required; and one sign of the times is the congestion in certain quarters of men who cannot or will not earn a living ... The unemployed are always with us, subsisting on the charity of free meals, shelters and casual wards, for which they feel no gratitude – and ready at any time of pressure to become the centre of an agitation.

(This couple was uniquely qualified to know the feelings of such people, be it understood.) The poverty and suffering all about them were to working people no abstract notion. Hyndman had made the daring estimate that one-quarter of London's population was living in poverty, only to be challenged by Charles Booth, a Liberal social reformer, who thereupon engaged a team of highly qualified invest-igators to make a detailed and scrupulously defined survey which, published after three years, precisely in 1889, revealed that not a quarter but almost one-third of Londoners – and nearly two-thirds in some East End districts – were living below subsistence level and going hungry.

SCOOP DRIVER.

Shocking as these stat-istics were, in themselves they meant little to the man in the street – the unemployed, the low-paid factory hand, the sweat-shop and the home worker – compared with everyday experience. The reality was very close and very painful. One has only to read Thorne's description of the children's soup kitchen organised in the Barking Road on Sunday mornings by the men and women of Canning Town to realise how that reality hurt:

> A more pitiable, heartbreaking sight than those poor ill-clothed children, coming along in the cold and biting winds, cannot be imagined. Sweet, tender young things, they were like ravenous wolves ... This sort of thing was breeding rebels and opponents of a system that permitted the poor to starve ...

Later, when reflecting upon the purpose of the New Unionism which he had founded, he observed:

> It was the lives of our people and their bread and butter we were thinking of. We were struggling to lift ourselves out of the slime of poverty into the fresh air of freedom.

This brings one to the nature of the leadership of that movement. There can be no denying that they were people of a special stamp and exceptional character. No matter how or why in later life they took to

SCOOP-DRIVER.

different paths – different from each other and different from the ways they chose at this period when none of them was yet 35 years of age – they all gave themselves heart and soul to the battle for their kind to live as decent human beings, entitled to work, to leisure and to the enjoyment of life.

It was not easy, in the same way as things are not easy today for the trade unionist. Speaking in our own time Raymond Williams said:

> All the big things are against us, but within what is not only a very powerful but also exceptionally unstable social and cultural order there are forces moving of which nobody can predict the outcome.

And who would expect, he asked,

> in our sort of world that it should be easier for him or her than for our brother and sister predecessors?

It was a stroke of genius on the part of those predecessors to have perceived, in the face of all previous experience and despite the inherent difficulties, that the social, economic and political climate favoured the launching of a union for men and women in the most diverse occupations, without any specific skills, more often than not employed in unpleasant, discontinuous and poorly paid work, accustomed to consider themselves hardly fitted to become trade unionists, yet with the inalienable rights,

THIS ADDRESS

(Together with a Watch and Chain)

Has been Presented to

WILLIAM THORNE

UNITY IS

STRENGTH.

General Secretary of the National Union of Gasworkers and
General Labourers of Great Britain & Ireland,

BY THE

Workmen of No. 3 Shift,

CARBONIZING DEPARTMENT, BECKTON GASWORKS,

As a humble token in recognition of the invaluable
services he has rendered to the Gasworkers of the
United Kingdom, and to the Cause of Labour
generally.

A CHAMPION OF THE RIGHTS OF LABOUR

from his Boyhood, his Untiring Energy, his Manly
Courage, his Earnest Advocacy, and his Honesty of
Purpose in the Cause of Trades Unionism, has
gained for him the admiration and respect of all
ranks in the Army of Labour.

On behalf of the Committee,

J. MACK, Treasurer.

OWEN CRUMMEY, Secretary.

the needs and the personal dignity which deserved to be as highly respected and as stoutly defended as those of anyone else.

No less inspired and certainly more astonishing was the notion of basing this new movement upon the single and simple demand for more humane hours of work. Exactly why the leaders should have hit upon and stuck to that as their prime cause remains today an unanswerable question. It also remains deeply impressive.

Those predecessors of ours have earned the undying gratitude of all later generations of trade unionists who salute the strength of purpose and the force of personality which led to the triumph of the New Unionism a hundred years ago. In particular those qualities in Will Thorne.

After the mass meeting held in Battersea on 17 July to celebrate the founding of the union and its victory in obtaining the eight-hour day, the newly introduced Number Three Shift in the carbonising department of the Beckton gasworks presented Thorne with a silver watch and addressed him thus:

> A champion of the rights of labour. From his Boyhood, his Untiring Energy, his Manly Courage, his Earnest Advocacy, and his Honesty of Purpose in the Cause of Trade Unionism, had gained for him the admiration and respect of all ranks of the Army of Labour.

And you cannot say fairer than that.

Sources

P = pamphlet, UT = unpublished thesis

Barnes, George, *From Workshop to War Cabinet*, Jenkins 1924.
Bédarida, François, *Will Thorne*, Fayard, Paris 1987.
Board of Trade, *Strikes and Lockouts, 1888*, HMSO 1889.
Claise, Jacqueline, *William Thorne; Campaign for West Ham South 1906* (UT Manchester 1982).
Clegg, H.A., *General Union*, Blackwell 1954, *General Union in a Changing Society*, Blackwell 1964; with Alan Fox and A.F. Thompson, *A History of British Trade Unions since 1889*, Vol. I, 1889-1910, OUP 1964.
Cole, G.D.H., *John Burns*, Gollancz 1943 (P).
Dictionary of Labour Biography, Macmillan Vol.I 1972, David Martin, 'Will Thorne'; Vol. IV 1977, A.J. Topham, 'Ben Tillett'; Vol. V 1979, Kenneth Brown, 'John Burns'; Barbara Nield, 'Pete Curran'.
Dictionary of National Biography 1941-1959, OUP 1959.
Dodds, George, 'A Day at the Westminster Gas Works', *Days at the Factories*, Charles Knight 1843.
Duffy, A.E.P., 'New Unionism in Britain 1889-1890', *Economic History Review*, December 1961.
Grant, Betty, *Beckton's Struggles*, Beckton Branch of the Communist Party 1955.
Grubb, Arthur Page, *John Burns*, Edward Dalton 1908.
Hobsbawm, E.J., *Labouring Men*, Weidenfeld & Nicolson 1968.
Jefferys, James, *The Story of the Engineers 1800-1945*, AEU 1945.

The Air of Freedom

Kapp, Yvonne, *Eleanor Marx*. Vol. I *Family Life*, Vol. II *The Crowded Years*, Lawrence & Wishart 1972 and 1976; Virago 1979.

Kent, William, *John Burns*, William & Norgate 1950.

Mann, Tom, *Memoirs*, Labour Publishing Co. 1923; *What a Compulsory Eight-Hour Day Means to the Workers* (1886) Pluto 1972 (P); *The Eight Hours Movement*, William Reeves, 1891 (P); with Ben Tillett, *New Trade Unionism*, Green & McAllan 1890 (P).

Mannion, Herbert, 'I was in a Gas Works', *Penny Magazine*, 1842, Vol. XI pp. 81-8.

Marriott, John, *London over the Border: Industry and Culture in West Ham* (UT Cambridge 1984).

Matthews, Derek, *The London Gasworks: A Technical, Commercial and Labour History to 1914* (UT Hull 1984).

Mills, Mary, *Profit-sharing in the South Metropolitan Gas Company* (UT Thames Polytechnic 1983); *Union Militancy 1889-1914* (UT Thames Polytechnic 1977).

Milne-Bailey, W., *Trade Union Documents*, G. Bell & Sons 1929.

Mitchell, B.R. and Deane, P., *Abstract of British Historical Statistics*, CUP 1962.

National Union of Gasworkers and General Labourers of Great Britain and Ireland, *Half-Yearly Reports and Balance Sheets 1889-1896; Annual Delegate Conference Reports 1890-1894 Rule Book 1890*.

National Union of General and Municipal Workers, *Souvenir Volumes for 1929, 1939 and 1949 (P). Jubilee 1889-1939*. Newcastle-upon-Tyne. P.

Radice, E.A. and G.H., *Will Thorne*, Allen & Unwin 1974.

Royal Commission on Labour, *Examination of Witnesses*,, HMSO 1894.

Society for the Study of Labour History, *Bulletin*, Vols 35, 36, 49.

Thompson, E.P., 'Homage to Tom Macquire' in Asa Briggs and John Saville (eds), *Essays in Labour History*, Macmillan 1960.

Thorne, Will, *My Life's Battles*, George Newnes n.d. (1925).

Tillett, Ben, *Memoirs and Reflections*, John Long 1931.

Sources

Torr, Dona, *Tom Mann*, Lawrence & Wishart 1936 (P);
    Tom Mann and His Times, Lawrence & Wishart 1956.

TUC *Reports* 1890-1897.

Webb, Sidney and Beatrice, *Industrial Democracy*,
    Longmans Green 1897; *A History of Trade Unionism*,
    trade union edition 1919.

Webb, Sidney and Cox, Harold, *The Eight Hours' Day*,
    Walter Scott 1891.

Whitaker's Almanack, 1889, 1892.

Williams, Trevor, *A History of the British Gas Industry*,
    OUP 1981.